Third Edition

CLEAR SPEECH

Pronunciation and Listening Comprehension in North American English

Judy B. Gilbert

Student's Book

CAMBRIDGE UNIVERSITY PRESS
Cambridge, New York, Melbourne, Madrid, Cape Town, Singapore, São Paulo, Delhi

Cambridge University Press
32 Avenue of the Americas, New York, NY 10013–2473, USA

www.cambridge.org
Information on this title: www.cambridge.org/9780521543545

First published 2005
10th printing 2008

Printed in Hong Kong, China, by Golden Cup Printing Company Limited

A catalog record for this publication is available from the British Library

Library of Congress Cataloging in Publication Data
Gilbert, Judy B. (Judy Bogen)
Clear speech : pronunciation and listening comprehension in North
American English : student's book / Judy B. Gilbert. – [3rd ed.].
p. cm.
ISBN 978-0-521-54354-5 (pbk. : alk. paper)
1. English language – Textbooks for foreign speakers. 2. English
language – Spoken English – United States – Problems, exercises, etc.
3. English language – Spoken English – Canada – Problems, exercises,
etc.4. English language – United States – Pronunciation – Problems,
exercises, etc. 5. English language – Canada – Pronunciation – Problems,
exercises, etc. 6. Listening – Problems, exercises, etc. I. Title.
PE1128.G52 2005
428.3'4 – dc22   2004057008

ISBN 978-0-521-54354-5 Student's Book   ISBN 978-0-521-54356-9 Audio Cassettes
ISBN 978-0-521-54355-2 Teacher's Resource Book ISBN 978-0-521-54357-6 Audio CDs

Book design and art direction: Adventure House, NYC
Layout services: Page Designs International

All illustrations done by Adam Hurwitz except page 28, which was done by Judy B. Gilbert; pages 77 *(bottom)*,
85 *(top)*, 90 *(middle)*, 119 *(bottom)*, 121 *(bottom)*, 140, 141, 143 *(top)*, 146 *(bottom)*, 156 *(bottom)*, which were
done by Judith Alderman; and pages 41, 47, 48, 51, 73, 93, 100, 114, 121, 122, 127, 135, which were done by
Andrew Shiff. Photographs on pages 140 and 141 were done by Paper Crane Design.

On page 37, "The Hippopotamus," in *I'm a Stranger Here Myself*, by Ogden Nash, 1938, Little, Brown and Co.
Reprinted by permission of Curtis Brown, Ltd. Copyright 1935 by Ogden Nash. Also in *Collected Poems*, by
Ogden Nash, Andre Deutsch Ltd.
Audio production by Richard LePage & Associates. "Bright Road" by Russ Gilman from his CD, *Back to the
Barrelhouse*.

To Jerry

Contents

Plan of the book .... *vi*

Acknowledgments .... *viii*

Letter to the student .... *ix*

Letter to the teacher .... *x*

Clear listening test .... *xiii*

Clear speaking test .... *xvii*

Key to sound symbols .... *xviii*

Syllables

Unit 1   Syllables **2**

Vowels and Word Stress

Unit 2   Vowels and vowel rules **10**

Unit 3   Word stress and vowel length **18**

Unit 4   Word stress and vowel clarity **25**

Unit 5   Word stress patterns **34**

Sentence Focus

Unit 6   Sentence focus: Emphasizing content words **44**

Unit 7   Sentence focus: De-emphasizing structure words **50**

Unit 8   Choosing the focus word **59**

Unit 9   Emphasizing structure words **69**

Consonants

Unit 10   Continuants and stops: /s/ and /t/ **76**

Unit 11   Continuants and stops: /r/ and /d/, /l/ and /d/ **84**

Unit 12   Voicing **97**

Unit 13   Voicing and syllable length **109**

Unit 14   Sibilants **119**

Thought Groups

Unit 15   Thought groups _____ **129**

Appendices

A   Parts of the mouth _____ **139**

B   Tongue shapes for /s/ and /z/, /t/ and /d/, /r/, /l/, /θ/ and /ð/ ____ **140**

C   More consonant work _____ **142**
      Part 1   /r/ and /l/
      Part 2   /n/ and /l/
      Part 3   /v/ and /w/
      Part 4   /v/ and /b/
      Part 5   /f/ and /p/
      Part 6   /θ/ and /t/
      Part 7   Silent -t- and reduced -t-
      Part 8   Aspiration
      Part 9   Practice with linking

D   Advanced tasks _____ **163**
      Part 1   Word stress
      Part 2   Sentence focus
      Part 3   Thought groups

E   How often do the vowel rules work? _____ **173**

Track listing for Student Audio CD _____ **174**

Plan of the book

Unit	Featured Topics	Music of English	Vowel Work
1 Syllables	Introducing syllables Counting syllables Syllable number in past and present tense verbs Silent letters	*How do you spell "ease"? E - A - S - E.* *How do you spell "easy"? E - A - S - Y.* *What does "easy" mean? "Easy" means "not hard."*	
2 Vowels and vowel rules	Alphabet vowel sounds The Two Vowel Rule Relative vowel sounds The One Vowel Rule Contrasting alphabet vowel sounds and relative vowel sounds	*Did you say "hope" or "hop"? I said "hope." H - O - P - E.*	
3 Word stress and vowel length	Stressed syllables Rules for stress and vowel length The Two Vowel Rule and One Vowel Rule for multi-syllable words	*Excuse me. Where's the bank? It's on the corner of Oater Road and Selling Street.*	
4 Word stress and vowel clarity	Clear vowels Schwa Contrasting clear and reduced vowels Stress rules for vowel length and vowel clarity Identifying stress in multi-syllable words	*What are you studying? Economics.*	The letters -y- and -w- as vowel sounds Linking vowels with an off-glide
5 Word stress patterns	Listening to stress patterns Stress rule for two-syllable words Stress rules for word endings Stress rule for two-syllable verb forms Stress in compound nouns	*Do they suspect him? Yes, he's a suspect.*	The spelling -ow- pronounced /α^w/ as in "cow." The spelling -ew- pronounced /u^w/ as in "new." Linking vowels with an off-glide
6 Sentence focus: Emphasizing content words	Emphasis in sentences Sentence focus Focus and content words Focus Rules 1 and 2 Emphasizing focus words	*You look confused! That's because I lost my glasses.*	Review: Linking vowels with off-glides
7 Sentence focus: De-emphasizing structure words	Focus and structure words Focus Rule 3 Contractions and reductions		The spelling -igh- pronounced /α^y/ as in "night" The spelling -oo- pronounced /u^w/ as in "moon"
8 Choosing the focus word	Focus at the beginning of a conversation Focus after the beginning of a conversation Disagreeing and correcting Using focus words to check information	*You buy books at the library. No, you borrow books at the library. Our copier isn't working. What's not working?*	The vowel sound /ɔ/ as in "saw"

Unit	Featured Topics	Music of English	Vowel Work
9 **Emphasizing structure words**	Emphasizing structure words Focus Rule 7 Review of Focus Rules	*Our specialties are steak and lobster. Terrific! I'll have steak and lobster.*	Different vowel sounds for the letter -a- The contrast between /ɔ/ and /ɑ/
10 **Continuants and stops: /s/ and /t/**	Introducing continuants and stops Saying /s/ and /t/ Singular and plural words	*Did you say "minute"?* *Did you say "minutes"?*	Practicing vowels with /s/ and /t/
11 **Continuants and stops: /r/ and /d/, /l/ and /d/**	Saying /r/ and /d/ The sound combination /r/ + /d/ Past and present tense verbs Saying /l/ and /d/ The sound combination /l/ + /d/ Contractions with final /l/ and /d/	*What color is rust? Usually orange.* *What color is dust? Usually gray.* *Did she succeed? No, quite the opposite. She failed.*	Using the Vowel Rules with /r/, /d/, and /l/ Practicing vowels with /r/, /d/, and /l/
12 **Voicing**	Introducing voicing Saying /s/ and /z/ Saying /f/ and /v/ Voiced and voiceless sounds for the spelling -th-	*That's amazing, isn't it?*	The vowel sound /ɔʸ/ as in "boy" and "coin"
13 **Voicing and syllable length**	Introducing voicing and syllable length Rule for voicing and syllable length Final voiced and voiceless continuants Final voiced and voiceless stops		The spelling -ou- pronounced /ɑʷ/ as in "house"
14 **Sibilants**	Introducing sibilants Contrasting /s/ and /ʃ/ Contrasting /z/ and /ʒ/ Contrasting /s/ and /θ/ Contrasting /ʃ/ and /tʃ/ Contrasting /dʒ/ and /y/ Sibilants and the number of syllables	*I'd like six oranges, and two wedges of cheese. Do you want large oranges, or small ones?*	Difficult vowel contrasts
15 **Thought groups**	Introducing thought groups Signaling the end of a thought group with a pause Signaling the end of a thought group with a falling pitch Thought Group Rules 1 and 2 Either/or questions Series of items Summary of focus and thought groups		

Acknowledgments

This book could not have been possible without the generous help of many people:

Thanks to colleagues who were generously responsive to my requests for advice: William Acton, Janet Anderson-Hsieh, Barbara Bradford, Tamikazu Date, Nancy Hilty, James Kirchner, Kazuhiko Matsuno, Carole Mawson, Barbara Seidlhofer, Elcio C. A. Souza, Setsuko Toyama, and Ann Wennerstrom.

Thanks to teachers who gave time and thought to the essential evaluating and/or testing of various raw drafts and to answering my many follow-up questions: Angela Albano, Francis Allegretti, Mary Althouse, Noelle Anderson, Ann Boyd, Brock Brady, Lucia Buttaro, Dorothy Chun, Karen Steffen Chung, Elsie Cooper, Stephanie Cross, Jessie Farrington, Judy Coppock Gex, Susan Gould, Julia Gribble, Nancy Hilty, Linda Hively, Brian Holliday, Phyllis Kaplan, Reverend James Kathol, James Kirchner, Yuko Kondo, Joanna Koulouriotis, Joan Kyle-Jones, Gunta Jurburgs, Joyce Mandell, Kazuhiko Matsuno, Peter Matteson, Carole Mawson, Bet Mesmer, Frank Mitchell, Beverly Price, Kathleen Rathbun, Cheryl Rowan, Jonghee Shadix, Katherine Sleep, Elcio C. A. Souza, Shari Tanck, Gail Tiessen, and Edith Uber.

Thanks to Olle Kjellin for his brilliant work on the theory and practice of choral repetition, and to William Acton for his unique insights into kinesthetic teaching of rhythm and intonation.

Thanks to Dorothy Cribbs, for developing the original widened vowel font; Ames Kanemoto, for making and photographing the tongue position models, and for developing the concept of shrinking letters for continuants; and Judith Alderman, for drawing the tongue positions from the back.

Thanks to my editors: Rob Freire, who with tact and intelligence helped me think through many complicated problems; and Jane Mairs, who ably supervised the overall project. Also, for their dedicated professionalism, thanks to Heather McCarron (Project Editor), Don Williams (Compositor), and Rich LePage (Audio Engineer).

For Jerry, thanks.

Letter to the student

This book is designed to help you make the most efficient use of your time as you learn to pronounce English better.

You probably want to learn how to pronounce the sounds of English more clearly. I think the most useful way to practice these sounds is by practicing the rhythm and melody of spoken English.

We all learn about the rhythm and melody of our own language when, as babies, we first begin to listen to others speak. Later, when we begin learning a new language, we automatically transfer this rhythm to the new language we are learning. But speaking a new language with the wrong rhythm makes it hard to say the sounds clearly, no matter how much you practice them. In fact, the more you practice with the wrong rhythm, the more your mistakes become fixed. A more efficient way to learn to speak clearly in English is to practice short sentences until you can say them easily, with the right rhythm and melody – the right "music." This will help make the sounds perfect.

This book will help you to speak more clearly and will also help you to understand what others are saying to you. You will learn, for example, what parts of a sentence are most important and how to help your listener hear those important parts. You will also learn ways to guess the pronunciation of a written word, even if you have never heard it pronounced before. All of this will enable you to communicate more easily and more clearly in English.

I hope that you enjoy learning with *Clear Speech*.

Judy B. Gilbert

Letter to the teacher

Clear Speech, Third Edition, concentrates on rhythm, stress, and intonation because improvement in these aspects of pronunciation can do the most good in improving both listening comprehension and clarity of speech. Individual speech sounds, however, are also significant, and are therefore covered throughout the book.

New features

In response to feedback received from teachers over the years, I have made seven important changes in this Third Edition:

1 Attention to vowels: Vowel quality has been upgraded to high-priority status. This has been done through the introduction of "de-coding" rules for spelling, to help students guess how a printed word should be pronounced. These rules are presented in Units 2 and 3 with ten basic vowel sounds. The Vowel Work sections that come at the end of the units that follow reinforce these rules and also introduce new vowel sounds and spellings.

2 Attention to listening comprehension: More listening activities have been included throughout the book. These help students develop listening comprehension skills and prepare them for the speaking exercises that follow.

3 Additional flexibility: The sequence of topics has been rearranged to provide more thorough practice of rhythm and intonation throughout the book. In order for you to adjust to the proficiency level and specific needs of a particular class, optional work at a higher level is provided in the appendices. Additional work on consonants is also provided in the appendices. These additional activities address consonant contrasts that cause problems for specific language backgrounds.

4 "Music of English" boxes: These activities give students an opportunity to personally "own" a short sequence of English syllables. Ownership of each sequence comes by way of "Quality Repetition." Students listen to a piece of spoken language and practice saying it with the same melody, thereby learning the sequence like a little song. Once the "song" becomes automatic, it can be used as raw material to analyze the crucial characteristics of spoken English. Old-fashioned repetition practice is boring, but true Quality Repetition gives students a momentum of confidence that is the opposite of boring. Further explanation of this method is included in the Teacher's Resource Book.

5 Sentence focus: The concept of sentence focus has been presented in a clearer way, and the topic has been more securely integrated into the work with thought groups.

6 Graphics and mouth drawings: New graphics are used throughout the book to provide visual representations of important pronunciation features, such as voicing, linking, and syllable length.

Colored screens are used to show students how a word sounds:

- Extra-wide letters show that a vowel is extra long.

   ban**a**na

- Schwa symbols show when a vowel is reduced.

   atəm

- Diminishing letters show how a continuant sound continues.

   bussss

- Vibrating letters show that a consonant is voiced.

   bu**zzzz**

Also new to this edition are original drawings and photos of the mouth viewed from the back. This perspective of the mouth shows how air flows, looking in the direction in which people actually think of their tongue.

7 Student Audio CD: An audio CD containing over one third of the full class audio program has been included in the Student's Book. For a list of the activities included on the Student Audio CD, refer to page 174.

Activity types

The following are some of the specific kinds of activities you will find in *Clear Speech,* Third Edition.

Clear Listening and Clear Speaking Tests: One or both of these tests can provide information about skill areas that need improvement. The teacher's version of the Clear Listening Test, with directions as well as analysis information and a student Pronunciation Profile form, is in the Teacher's Resource Book.

Pair work: Pair work activities provide a communicative challenge and give students – even in very large classes – the opportunity to practice speaking and hearing English. Pair work provides the immediate feedback so important to motivation. Moreover, it places more responsibility for learning where it belongs – with the student.

While students work together in pairs, you can circulate among them, giving help on a more personal basis. To provide variety, the pair work activities can be used as a listening exercise or as a quiz, with the teacher playing the part of Student A and the whole class playing Student B. Alternately, one student can be Student A and the rest of the class can be Student B.

Dictation: Taking dictation alerts students to areas of listening perception that still need improvement. You can read aloud from the Teacher's Resource Book or use the audio program. Interest can be enhanced by using dictation material from the students' own fields of study or work or from current topical subjects.

Rhythm practice: While rhythm is taught mainly through the the "Music of English" boxes, there are also brief pieces of light poetry throughout the book, which have been included to encourage a sense of the flow of English rhythm. You may find other poetry (e.g., the lyrics of songs) more suited to your particular students. The class can listen to the teacher or the audio, then recite the poem as a group or as separate groups saying alternate lines. Rhythm practice is most effective when physical activity is included, such as marking time by tapping the table or moving the body in some way. The Teacher's Resource Book suggests a variety of physical activities to reinforce intonational emphasis and timing.

Listening activities: "Which word do you hear?" and "Which word is different?" activities help students learn to recognize particular sounds and stress patterns. These listening tasks also help prepare students to later produce the sounds and stress patterns they have learned.

Activity selection

This book was designed to be used in a wide range of teaching situations; therefore, you should feel free to choose those activities that are most appropriate for your students. You may also wish to shorten some activities if further practice is unnecessary. If your students are advanced, you can choose more demanding tasks from Appendix D: Advanced Tasks. You can also choose tasks from Appendix C: More Consonant Work, to address the particular difficulties that your students may have with English consonant sounds.

Teacher's Resource Book

This companion book can enhance the teaching of the text because it provides practical explanations of the rationale for each lesson, useful classroom procedures, answer keys, ready-made quizzes, and lectures for listening practice.

Many teachers have helped me plan the Third Edition of *Clear Speech* and make it more teachable. I hope that you find using it with your students to be interesting and professionally rewarding.

Judy B. Gilbert

Clear listening test

How you hear English is closely connected with how you speak English.

Part 1   *Consonants* [10 points]

Listen. You will hear either sentence **a** or sentence **b**. Circle the letter of the sentence you hear.

1. a. Do you want everything?
   b. Do you wash everything?

2. a. They saved old bottles.
   b. They save old bottles.

3. a. She loves each child.
   b. She loved each child.

4. a. We'll put it away.
   b. We've put it away.

5. a. He spills everything.
   b. He spilled everything.

6. a. Does she bring her card every day?
   b. Does she bring her car every day?

7. a. What does "leave" mean?
   b. What does "leaf" mean?

8. a. Who'll ask you?
   b. Who'd ask you?

9. a. We wash all of them.
   b. We watch all of them.

10. a. He put the tickets away.
    b. He put the ticket away.

11. a. Is this the long road?
    b. Is this the wrong road?

Part 2   *Vowels*   [10 points]

Listen. You will hear either sentence **a** or sentence **b**. Circle the letter of the sentence you hear.

1. a. Did you bring the bat?
   b. Did you bring the bait?

2. a. I prefer this test.
   b. I prefer this taste.

3. a. It's a good bet.
   b. It's a good bit.

4. a. It's on the track.
   b. It's on the truck.

5. a. The men worked hard.
   b. The man worked hard.

6. a. How do you spell "scene"?
   b. How do you spell "sin"?

7. a. How do you spell "luck"?
   b. How do you spell "lock"?

8. a. We used a map.
   b. We used a mop.

9. a. Is John coming?
   b. Is Joan coming?

10. a. Everybody left.
    b. Everybody laughed.

11. a. I ran to school every day.
    b. I run to school every day.

Part 3   *Syllables*   [10 points]

Listen and write the number of syllables in each word.

1. easy   2
2. closet
3. sport
4. clothes
5. simplify
6. frightened

7. opened
8. first
9. caused
10. Wednesday
11. arrangement

Part 4 _Word stress_ [10 points]

Listen. In each word, one syllable is stressed more than the others. Underline the stressed syllable in each word.

1. <u>a</u>rrangement
2. political
3. photograph
4. photography
5. Canadian
6. geography

7. Europe
8. information
9. economy
10. economic
11. participating

Part 5 _Emphasizing focus words_ [20 points]

Listen to the following dialogue. In each sentence, one word is emphasized more than the others. Underline the emphasized word in each sentence.

A: Do you think food in this country is <u>expensive</u>?
B: Not really.
A: Well, I think it's expensive.
B: That's because you eat in restaurants.
A: Where do you eat?
B: At home.
A: You must like to cook.
B: Actually, I never cook.
A: So what do you eat?
B: Usually, just cheese.
A: That's awful!

Part 6 _De-emphasizing with contractions and reductions_ [20 points]

Listen. You will hear each sentence two times. Write the missing words in the blanks.

1. Do you think _____she's OR she is_____ in her room?
2. _____ you ask?
3. _____ work good?
4. Please _____ the information.
5. _____ want food?

6. How _____ you been here?

7. _____ Matt done lately?

8. Why _____ come so early?

9. _____ they gone?

10. We'd like some _____ vegetables.

11. They'll need _____ glasses.

Part 7   *Thought groups*   [20 points]

Listen. You will hear sentence **a** or sentence **b**. After you hear the sentence two times, answer the question that follows.

1. a. John said, "My father is in the kitchen."
   b. "John," said my father, "is in the kitchen."

   Question: Who was speaking?   _____ *my father* _____

2. a. The president shouted, "That reporter is lying!"
   b. "The president," shouted that reporter, "is lying!"

   Question: Who shouted?   _____

3. a. She wants pineapples.
   b. She wants pie and apples.

   Question: What does she want?   _____

4. a. Would you like a Super Salad?
   b. Would you like a soup or salad?

   Question: What were you offered?   _____

5. a. We used wooden matches to start the fire.
   b. We used wood and matches to start the fire.

   Question: What was used to start the fire?   _____

6. a. He sold his houseboat and car.
   b. He sold his house, boat, and car.

   Question: How many things did he sell?   _____

Clear speaking test

Practice saying this dialogue until you are comfortable with it. Then record it, speaking as naturally as possible.

Two University Students Meet

A: [1] Excuse me. Where's the library?

B: It's on the corner of Main Street and Selling Road.

A: [3] Sorry, did you say Selling or Ceiling?

B: Selling. It's directly ahead of you, about 2 blocks.

A: [5] Thanks. I need to buy some books for my classes.

B: Oh, then you need the bookstore. You can't buy books at the [7] library. You can only borrow them there.

A: I guess I confused the words. They're different in my language.

B: [9] I know how it is. I get mixed up with Spanish words that sound like English words, but have different meanings.

A: [11] Are you studying Spanish?

B: Yes, it's going to be my major. What are you studying?

A: [13] I'm studying English now, but my major will be economics.

B: Really? My brother wanted to study economics. He took the [15] entrance exam for that department just last week.

A: Did he succeed?

B: [17] No, quite the opposite. He failed.

A: That's too bad.

B: [19] Oh, it's OK. He would've had to study statistics, and he hated that idea. Anyway, he changed his mind, and now he plans to [21] study music.

A: That's great! Does he want to compose or perform?

B: [23] Both. He wants to compose and perform. He arranges programs for musicians, but he also plays classical guitar.

A: [25] Well, I wish him a lot of luck. And good luck to you, too. It was nice talking.

Key to sound symbols

VOWELS			
Key words	*Clear Speech*	*Cambridge Dictionary of American English/* International Phonetic Alphabet	Your dictionary
cake, mail, pay	/eʸ/	/eɪ/	
pan, bat, hand	/æ/	/æ/	
tea, feet, key	/iʸ/	/iː/	
ten, well, red	/ɛ/	/e/	
ice, pie, night	/ɑʸ/	/aɪ/	
is, fish, will	/ɪ/	/ɪ/	
cone, road, know	/oʷ/	/oʊ/	
top, rock, stop	/ɑ/	/ɑ/	
blue, school, new, cube, few	/uʷ/	/uː/	
cup, us, love	/ʌ/	/ʌ/ ɨ	
house, our, cow	/ɑʷ/	/aʊ/	
saw, talk, applause	/ɔ/	/ɔː/	
boy, coin, join	/ɔʸ/	/ɔɪ/	
put, book, woman	/ʊ/	/ʊ/	
alone, open, pencil, atom, ketchup	/ə/	/ə/	

CONSONANTS

Key words	Clear Speech	Cambridge Dictionary of American English/ International Phonetic Alphabet	Your dictionary
bid, jo**b**	/b/	/b/	
do, fee**d**	/d/	/d/	
food, sa**f**e	/f/	/f/	
go, do**g**	/g/	/g/	
home, be**h**ind	/h/	/h/	
kiss, ba**ck**	/k/	/k/	
load, poo**l**	/l/	/l/	
man, plu**m**	/m/	/m/	
need, ope**n**	/n/	/n/	
pen, ho**p**e	/p/	/p/	
road, ca**r**d	/r/	/r/	
see, re**c**ent	/s/	/s/	
show, na**ti**on	/ʃ/	/ʃ/	
team, mee**t**	/t/	/t/	
choose, wa**tch**	/tʃ/	/tʃ/	
think, bo**th**	/θ/	/θ/	
this, fa**th**er	/ð/	/ð/	
visit, sa**v**e	/v/	/v/	
watch, a**w**ay	/w/	/w/	
yes, oni**o**n	/y/	/j/	
zoo, the**s**e	/z/	/z/	
bei**g**e, mea**s**ure	/ʒ/	/ʒ/	
jump, bri**dge**	/dʒ/	/dʒ/	

1 Syllables

A Introducing syllables ☐☐☐

The basic unit of English rhythm is the syllable. Listen.

☐	☐☐	☐☐☐
ease	easy	easily
care	careful	carefully
paint	painted	repainted
call	recall	recalling

B Which word is different?

Listen. You will hear three words. Mark the column for the word
that is different.

	A	B	C	
1.	....	....	✔.............	(fish, fish, fishy)
2.	....	....	....	
3.	....	....	....	
4.	....	....	....	
5.	....	....	....	
6.	....	....	....	
7.	....	....	....	
8.	....	....	....	

C Tapping the syllables ☐☐☐

Listen and repeat the words while tapping your hand or foot for each syllable.

☐	☐☐	☐☐☐	☐☐☐☐
one	seven	eleven	identify
two	sentence	direction	analysis
noun	focus	continue	It's important.
verb	eighteen	emphasis	He wants a book.
can't	cannot	syllable	I have to go.

D Which word do you hear?

Listen. Circle the word you hear.

□	□□
1. mess	(messy)
2. blow	below
3. prayed	parade
4. loud	aloud
5. sport	support
6. round	around
7. claps	collapse
8. clone	cologne
9. state	estate
10. squeeze	excuse

E Pair work: One or two syllables? □ □ □

Student A: Say one word from each pair of words.
Student B: Hold up one finger if the word has one syllable or
two fingers if the word has two syllables.

Take turns saying words. Do not always say the first word in each pair.

Examples

Student A: "Sunny."
Student B: (Hold up two fingers.)

Student A: "Red."
Student B: (Hold up one finger.)

□	□□
1. sun	– sunny
2. red	– ready
3. flow	– fellow
4. rose	– roses
5. steam	– esteem
6. paint	– painted
7. boss	– bosses
8. sport	– support
9. blow	– below
10. sleep	– asleep

F Extra syllable in past tense verbs ☐☐☐

Usually, when **-ed** is added to a verb to make it past tense, the number of syllables in the verb *does not* change. But with some verbs, adding **-ed** *does* add an extra syllable.

1 Listen to how **-ed** changes the following verbs.

Present Tense ⟶ Past Tense

☐	☐☐
rent	rented
plant	planted

2 Listen. Hold up one finger if you hear one syllable and two fingers if you hear two syllables.

fainted	landed	worked	caused	planned
laughed	added	folded	treated	counted
started	watched	closed	asked	cooked

Do you know the rule for when **-ed** is pronounced as an extra syllable? If not, work out the following puzzle.

3 *Puzzle:* The verbs in lists A and B below have an extra syllable in the past tense. How are they different from the verbs in lists C and D?

A	B	C	D
plant	land	work	wash
start	fold	live	walk
treat	add	save	cause
wait	raid	laugh	plan
heat	load	call	close
attract	record	arrange	contain

Clue: Look at how the verbs in list A and list B are spelled. What do all the verbs in list A have in common? What do all the verbs in list B have in common?

4 Can you figure out the rule for saying an extra syllable in the past tense? Write down what you think it is. Check your answer on the last page of this unit.

Rule: ....

G __Counting syllables in past tense verbs__ ☐ ☐ ☐

1 Listen. You will hear the present tense and the past tense of the following verbs. Write down the past tense of each verb.

Present Tense	Syllables	Past Tense	Syllables
1. paint	1	*painted*	*2*
2. clean	1		
3. need	1		
4. decide	2		
5. dislike	2		
6. prepare	2		
7. represent	3		
8. entertain	3		

2 Listen again and write the number of syllables in each past tense verb.

H *Pair work: Past or present?*

Student A: Say sentence **a** or **b**.
Student B: Say "Past" or "Present."

Take turns saying the sentences. Do not always choose sentence **a**.

Example

> Student A: "We wanted to buy a used car."
> Student B: "Past."

1. a. We want to buy a used car.
   b. We wanted to buy a used car.

2. a. We start by looking in the newspaper.
   b. We started by looking in the newspaper.

3. a. The doctors treat sick people.
   b. The doctors treated sick people.

4. a. We rent a house every summer.
   b. We rented a house every summer.

5. a. The teachers want a pay raise.
   b. The teachers wanted a pay raise.

6. a. They start at 8 o'clock.
   b. They started at 8 o'clock.

7. a. I intend to go shopping.
    b. I intended to go shopping.

8. a. People crowd into trains.
    b. People crowded into trains.

9. a. Children skate on the frozen lake.
    b. Children skated on the frozen lake.

10. a. They never visit the library.
    b. They never visited the library.

Silent letters

Some English words have letters that are silent. Silent letters can affect the number of syllables in a word. It is important that you pronounce words in English with the correct number of syllables.

1 Listen. Draw an X through the silent letters in these words.

□	□□	□□□	□□□□
walked	business	vegetable*	laboratory*
planned	several	interesting*	elementary*
closed	chocolate		
talked	Wednesday		
	every		
	family		

2 Read the words aloud at least two times.

J Dictation: How many syllables? □□□

Listen and write the sentences you hear. Then count the number of syllables in each sentence. You will hear each sentence two times.

Number of syllables

1. *He works in an interesting business*   *9*

2. _____   _____

3. _____   _____

4. _____   _____

5. _____   _____

---

* These are common pronunciations in North America, but some native speakers of English may say these words differently.

1 Listen to these sentences.

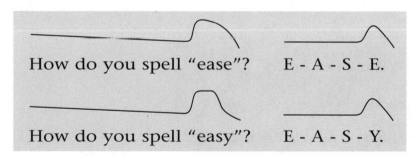

How do you spell "ease"? E - A - S - E.

How do you spell "easy"? E - A - S - Y.

2 Listen again. Say the sentences at least three times, or as many times as you need to be able to say them easily. Learn them like little songs.

L *Pair work: Asking about spelling*

Student A: Ask question **a** or question **b**.
Student B: Answer the question.
Student A: If the answer is wrong, repeat the question.

Take turns asking and answering.

Example

Student A: "How do you spell 'support'?"
Student B: "S - P - O - R - T."
Student A: "No. How do you spell 'support'?"
Student B: "S - U - P - P - O - R - T."

1. a. How do you spell "ease"? E - A - S - E.
   b. How do you spell "easy"? E - A - S - Y.

2. a. How do you spell "sport"? S - P - O - R - T.
   b. How do you spell "support"? S - U - P - P - O - R - T.

3. a. How do you spell "traffic"? T - R - A - F - F - I - C.
   b. How do you spell "terrific"? T - E - R - R - I - F - I - C.

4. a. How do you spell "squeeze"? S - Q - U - E - E - Z - E.
   b. How do you spell "excuse"? E - X - C - U - S - E.

5. a. How do you spell "boss"? B - O - S - S.
   b. How do you spell "bosses"? B - O - S - S - E - S.

6. a. How do you spell "close"? C - L - O - S - E.
   b. How do you spell "close it"? C - L - O - S - E   I - T.

M Music of English 🎵

1 Listen to the music of these sentences.

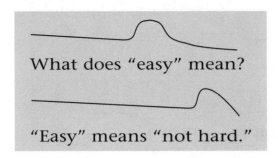

What does "easy" mean?

"Easy" means "not hard."

2 Listen again. Practice saying the sentences until you can say them easily.

N Pair work: Asking about meaning

Student A: Ask question **a** or question **b**.
Student B: Say the matching answer.

Take turns asking and answering.

Example

> Student A: "What does 'easy' mean?"
> Student B: "'Easy' means 'not hard.'"

1. a. What does "ease" mean?   "Ease" means "comfort."
   b. What does "easy" mean?   "Easy" means "not hard."

2. a. What does "need" mean?   "Need" means "must have."
   b. What does "needed" mean?   "Needed" is the past tense of "need."

3. a. What does "closed" mean?   The opposite of "open."
   b. What does "closet" mean?   A place to put things.

4. a. Where is the first?   At the beginning.
   b. Where is the forest?   In the mountains.

5. a. What does "traffic" mean?   Lots of cars.
   b. What does "terrific" mean? "Great!"

6. a. What does "cracked" mean?   Something like "broken."
   b. What does "correct" mean?   "Right."

O *Check yourself: Counting syllables* □□□

1 Listen. Write the number of syllables over the underlined words.

This is the <u>first</u> <u>city</u> they <u>visited</u> when they <u>traveled</u> here on <u>business</u>.

They were so <u>pleased</u> that they <u>decided</u> to stay <u>seven</u> extra days.

2 If you have a tape recorder, record yourself saying these sentences. Listen to hear how well you did.

P *Syllable number game* □□□

Divide into teams. In five minutes, how many foods can you think of that have one, two, three, or four syllables?

□	□□	□□□	□□□□
rice	ice cream	banana	asparagus
....	....	....	....
....	....	....	....
....	....	....	....
....	....	....	....

Another possible category: countries and cities.

□	□□	□□□	□□□□
France	Japan	Singapore	Argentina
....	....	....	....
....	....	....	....
....	....	....	....
....	....	....	....

Answer to Task F (page 4)

4 *Rule:* If the last sound of a regular verb is /t/ or /d/, the past tense has an extra syllable.

2 Vowels and vowel rules

A Introducing vowels

In English spelling, each vowel letter can be pronounced with different sounds. There are only five vowel letters, but there are many more vowel sounds. The most common pronunciations are the *alphabet vowel sounds* and the *relative vowel sounds*.

B Alphabet vowel sounds

Listen to the names of the English vowel letters.

   a, e, i, o, u

Sometimes vowel letters are pronounced like their letter names. These sounds are called the *alphabet vowel sounds*. The alphabet vowel sounds are pronounced with a small change in the sound at the end. This change is called the *off-glide*.

C The tongue in alphabet vowel sounds

1 Look at these pictures of the tongue pronouncing the alphabet vowel sound for each letter. The solid line in the picture shows where the tongue begins. The dotted line shows how the tongue moves for the off-glide at the end.

2 Listen to the alphabet vowel sounds while you look at each picture.

-a-

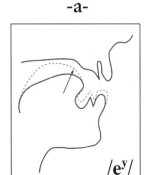

/e^y/

-e-

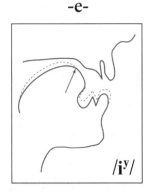

/i^y/

-i-

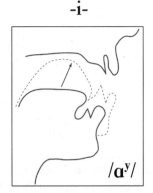

/ɑ^y/

-o-   -u-

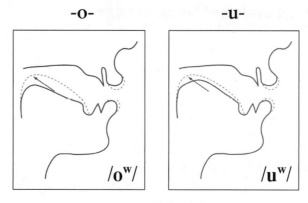

/oʷ/   /uʷ/

The lips in alphabet vowel sounds

The following pictures show how the lips change when the alphabet vowel sounds are being said.

Listen to the vowel sounds while you look at the pictures.

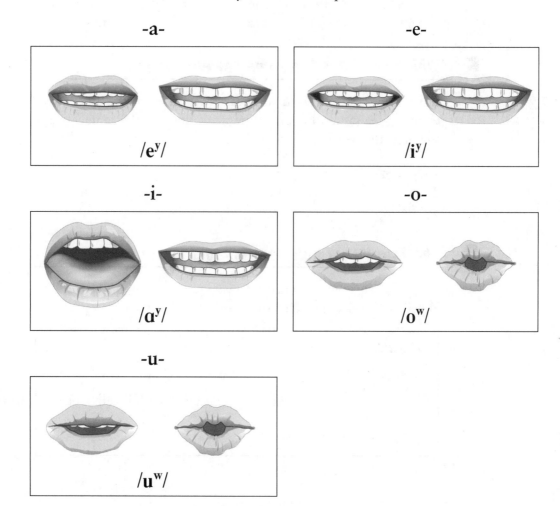

-a-   -e-

/eʸ/   /iʸ/

-i-   -o-

/aʸ/   /oʷ/

-u-

/uʷ/

E Listening to alphabet vowel sounds

1 Listen to the alphabet vowel sounds in these key words.

/e^y/	/i^y/	/ɑ^y/	/o^w/	/u^w/
cake	tea	ice	cone	blue

Note: In some words, the alphabet vowel sound for the letter -u- is pronounced /**yu**^{w}/, as in "cube." The sound /**u**^{w}/ as in "blue," however, is more common. In this book, the symbol /**u**^{w}/ will be used for both these pronunciations.

2 Listen to the alphabet vowel sounds in these other words.

/e^y/	/i^y/	/ɑ^y/	/o^w/	/u^w/
mail	leaf	lime	phone	tune
rain	steam	dine	coal	suit
train	breeze	file	froze	use
paid	feed	bite	coat	fume

F Which word has the same vowel sound?

Listen and write the word you hear. Then listen to the other two words in the same row. Circle the word that has the same vowel sound as the word you wrote.

1. ___tea___   (eat)   ate   4. _____   coat   cute
2. _____   place   rice   5. _____   name   time
3. _____   suit   so

G The Two Vowel Rule for alphabet vowel sounds

This rule helps predict when a vowel letter is pronounced with its alphabet vowel sound. The rule works for many words.*

> **The Two Vowel Rule**
>
> If there are TWO vowel letters in a one-syllable word:
>
> 1. The first vowel letter is pronounced with its alphabet vowel sound.
> 2. The second vowel letter is silent.

---

* Check Appendix E to see how often this vowel rule works.

H Practicing alphabet vowel sounds

Listen to the vowel sounds in these words. Repeat each word.

/eʸ/	/iʸ/	/aʸ/	/oʷ/	/uʷ/
change	teach	pie	boat	dues
main	mean	fine	chose	rude
save	sleep	twice	note	prunes
grapes	seat	dried	pose	fumes

I Relative vowel sounds

Vowel letters are not always pronounced with their alphabet vowel
sounds. Often a vowel letter is pronounced with a *relative vowel
sound*. This sound is related to the alphabet vowel sound, but it
has a different sound and there is no off-glide.

1 Listen to the relative vowel sounds in these key words.

/æ/	/ɛ/	/ɪ/	/ɑ/	/ʌ/
pan	ten	is	top	cut

2 Listen to the relative vowel sounds in these other words.

/æ/	/ɛ/	/ɪ/	/ɑ/	/ʌ/
back	jet	sip	lock	cup
fan	French	pin	pot	jump
half	leg	kick	flock	fun
clap	send	wrist	clock	gum

J Which word is different?

Listen. Mark the column for the word that is different. The word
that is different has a relative vowel sound.

	A	B	C	
1.	....	✔	....	(aid, add, aid)
2.	....	....	....	
3.	....	....	....	
4.	....	....	....	
5.	....	....	....	
6.	....	....	....	
7.	....	....	....	
8.	....	....	....	

K The One Vowel Rule for relative vowel sounds

This rule helps predict when a vowel letter is pronounced with a relative vowel sound. The rule works for many words.*

> **The One Vowel Rule**
>
> If there is only ONE vowel letter in a short word, it is pronounced with its relative vowel sound.

L Practicing relative vowel sounds

Listen to the vowel sounds in these words. Repeat each word.

/æ/	/ɛ/	/ɪ/	/ɑ/	/ʌ/
has	bed	his	stop	up
cat	send	pin	shop	run
man	men	fill	Tom	lunch
plan	tell	dig	Bob	plum
sack	red	fish	dock	luck

M Contrasting alphabet vowel sounds and relative vowel sounds

Listen and repeat these pairs of words.

Alphabet vowel sound		Relative vowel sound	
aid	/e^y/	add	/æ/
seat	/i^y/	set	/ɛ/
mice	/ɑ^y/	miss	/ɪ/
pine	/ɑ^y/	pin	/ɪ/
pike	/ɑ^y/	pick	/ɪ/
teen	/i^y/	ten	/ɛ/
hope	/o^w/	hop	/ɑ/
cheese	/i^y/	chess	/ɛ/
cute	/u^w/	cut	/ʌ/

---

* Check Appendix E to see how often this rule works.

N Guessing the pronunciation of a word

1 Read the words below. You may not know these words, but you can use the vowel rules to guess how the underlined letter is pronounced. Make a mark to show if the letter is pronounced with its alphabet vowel sound or its relative vowel sound.

	Alphabet vowel sound	Relative vowel sound
1. r<u>o</u>ve	✔	....
2. sp<u>a</u>n	....	....
3. v<u>i</u>ce	....	....
4. m<u>o</u>at	....	....
5. sl<u>ai</u>n	....	....
6. m<u>e</u>ld	....	....
7. st<u>i</u>nt	....	....
8. j<u>u</u>te	....	....

2 Listen to the words to see if you guessed the vowel sounds correctly.

O Listening to contrasting vowels in sentences

Listen to each sentence and circle the word you hear.

1. Did you say (**hope**)/ **hop**?
2. How do you spell **lease** / **less**?
3. What does **tape** / **tap** mean?
4. Did you **say** / **see** it?
5. I need a **pan** / **pen**.
6. Did you want **this** / **these**?
7. How do you spell **his** / **he's**?

P Music of English ♫♪

1 Listen to these sentences.

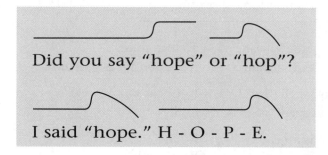

Did you say "hope" or "hop"?

I said "hope." H - O - P - E.

2 Listen again. Say the sentences at least three times, until you can say them smoothly and easily.

Unit 2 • 15

Q Pair work: Contrasting vowels

Student A: Say one word in the pair. Do not always choose the
first word.
Student B: Ask which word was said.
Student A: Answer and spell the word you said.

Take turns choosing a word to say.

Example

> Student A: "Hop."
> Student B: "Did you say 'hope' or 'hop'?"
> Student A: "I said 'hop.' H - O - P."

1. hope, hop
2. bead, bed
3. cute, cut
4. main, man
5. bite, bit
6. lame, lamb
7. goat, got
8. pine, pin

R Pair work: Contrasting vowels in sentences

Student A: Ask question **a** or **b**. Do not always choose question **a**.
Student B: Say the answer.
Student A: If the answer is incorrect, repeat the question.

Take turns asking the questions.

Example

> Student A: "What does 'fad' mean?"
> Student B: "A fashion for a short time."

1. a. What does "fade" mean?   To lose color.
   b. What does "fad" mean?   A fashion for a short time.

2. a. How do you spell "ice"?   I - C - E.
   b. How do you spell "is"?   I - S.

3. a. What shape is a bead?   Round.
   b. What shape is a bed?   Rectangular.

4. a. What does "cute" mean?   Attractive.
   b. What does "cut" mean?   To slice.

5. a. How do you spell "beast"?   B - E - A - S - T.
   b. How do you spell "best"?   B - E - S - T.

6. a. What's a pine?   A kind of tree.
   b. What's a pin?   Something with a sharp point.

S Check yourself: Alphabet vowel sounds and relative vowel sounds

1 Listen and repeat each sentence.

1. Raisins are dried grapes.
2. Prunes are dried plums.
3. The pin is stuck in the seat.
4. Clip this note to the box.

2 If you have a tape recorder, record yourself saying the sentences. Listen to your recording. Did you say the vowel sounds correctly?

T Dictation

Listen and write down the sentences you hear.

1. *Did you say teen or ten?*

2.

3.

4.

5.

3 Word stress and vowel length

A Stressed syllables

The vowel letter -a- appears three times in the word below. The second -a-, however, is larger and easier to see.

ban**a**na

1 Listen to the word and notice how the second -a- sounds different from the others.

In the second syllable the sound of the letter -a- is longer and easier to hear. This syllable is the *stressed syllable*.

2 Listen again.

ban**a**na

B Word stress and vowel length

The following rules will help you to identify the stressed syllable in English words.

Rules for Stress and Vowel Length

1. In every English word of more than one syllable, one syllable is stressed the most.

2. The vowel in the stressed syllable is extra long.

ban**a**na

C Listening for vowel length

1 Listen. Notice how the vowel in the stressed syllable is extra long.

C**a**nada   Jap**a**n   Ch**i**na   Am**e**rica   **E**ngland

2 Listen. Underline the stressed syllable.

<u>so</u>fa	ar<u>ound</u>	solution	beautiful
oven	event	arrangement	horrible
painting	arrange	pollution	en<u>e</u>rgy
London	Brazil	Atlanta	Ottawa
England	Berlin	Alberta	Washington

D Saying stressed syllables

Listen and repeat these words. Pay attention to the length of the stressed syllable.

□▭	▭□
remain	mainly
amaze	soapy
arrive	reason
arrange	training
explain	sailing

E Saying words with more than two syllables

Listen and repeat these words. Make sure that you lengthen the vowel in the stressed syllable.

□▭□	▭□□
attractive	principle
atomic	politics
arrangement	sensitive
electric	minister

F Pair work: Stress in acronyms

The last letter in an acronym usually gets the most stress.

1 Listen and notice how the last letter is stressed.

□▭
T V

□□▭
B B C

□□▭
U S A

2 Student A: Ask any question from the list.
Student B: Answer the question.

Take turns asking questions until all the questions are answered.

1.	What does "TV" mean?	Television.
2.	What does "UN" mean?	United Nations.
3.	What does "DC" mean?	District of Columbia (Washington, D.C.).
4.	What does "BC" mean?	British Columbia (Canada).
5.	What does "LA" mean?	Los Angeles.
6.	What does "USA" mean?	United States of America.
7.	What does "BBC" mean?	British Broadcasting Company.
8.	What does "CNN" mean?	Cable News Network.
9.	What does "CBC" mean?	Canadian Broadcasting Corporation.
10.	What does "CD" mean?	Compact disc.
11.	What does "IT" mean?	Information technology.

 **G** ## The Two Vowel Rule with multi-syllable words

In Unit 2 you studied the Two Vowel Rule in one-syllable words.
This same rule usually works for the stressed syllable of longer words.

> **The Two Vowel Rule for Multi-Syllable Words**
>
> If there are two vowel letters in the STRESSED syllable of a word:
>
> 1. The first vowel is pronounced with its alphabet sound.
> 2. The second vowel is silent.

Listen and repeat these words. Be sure to use an alphabet vowel sound in the stressed syllable. The stressed syllable is in bold.

/e^y/	/i^y/	/a^y/	/o^w/	/u^w/
cake	tea	ice	cone	blue
re**main**	re**peat**	a**live**	**soap**y	**Tues**day
e**rase**	de**lete**	in**side**	a**lone**	as**sume**
pa**rade**	re**treat**	pro**vide**	sup**pose**	intro**duce**
graceful	a**gree**ment	en**tire**ly	a**pproach**	con**fuse**
raisin	**rea**son	**price**less	**float**able	ex**cuse**

H The One Vowel Rule with multi-syllable words

The One Vowel Rule also works with many longer words.

> **The One Vowel Rule for Multi-Syllable Words**
>
> If there is only one vowel letter in the STRESSED syllable of
> a word, it is pronounced with its relative vowel sound.

Listen to the vowel sounds in the stressed syllable of these words.
Repeat each word, and be sure to use a relative vowel sound in
the stressed syllable.

/æ/	/ɛ/	/ɪ/	/ɑ/	/ʌ/
pan	ten	is	top	cut

attract	**rel**ative	**fill**ing	**stopp**ing	**Sun**day
practice	**sen**tence	**prin**ter	**cop**y	be**gun**
ex**am**ple	su**ggest**	**prin**ciple	**atom**ic	**thun**der
co**mmand**	e**lec**tric	**miss**ing	**tol**erance	**pun**ish
Saturday	ex**pen**sive	pre**dict**	**op**erate	a**bun**dant

I Music of English 🎵🎶

1 Listen to these sentences.

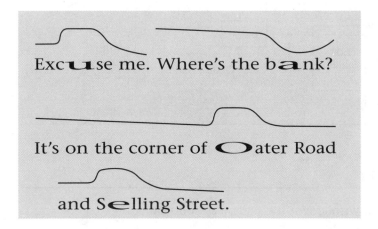

Exc**u**se me. Where's the b**a**nk?

It's on the corner of ◯ater Road

and S⊖lling Street.

2 Listen again. Practice saying the sentences until you can say
them easily.

J *Pair work: Map game*

1 Student A: Look at Map A on page 23.
   Student B: Look at Map B on page 24.

2 Student A: Ask the location of a place in the box below the map.
   Student B: Tell your partner where the place is located. Make
            sure to use words only. Do not use your hands to point.

3 Student A: Write the place in the correct location on your map.

Take turns asking questions. When your maps are complete, check
your answers. Did you write the place names in the correct locations?

Example

Student A: (Look at Map A.) "Excuse me. Where's the bank?"
Student B: (Look at Map B.) "It's on the corner of Oater Road and Selling Street."
Student A: (Write "bank" in the correct location on Map A.)

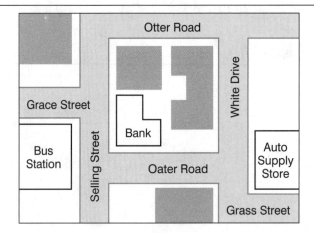

K *Dictation*

Listen and write down the sentences you hear.

1. *Please remain seated* ....

2. ....

3. ....

4. ....

5. ....

MAP A

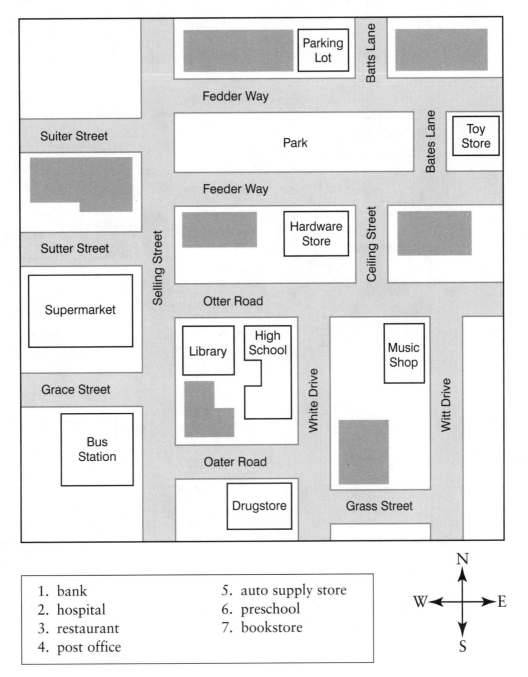

1. bank
2. hospital
3. restaurant
4. post office
5. auto supply store
6. preschool
7. bookstore

MAP B

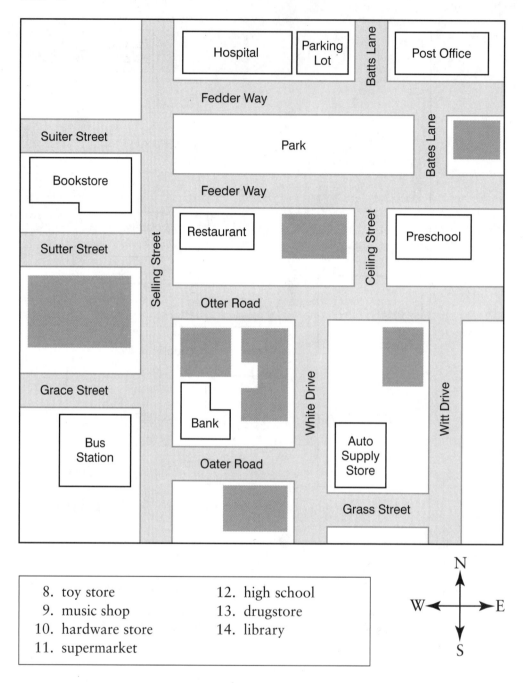

8. toy store
9. music shop
10. hardware store
11. supermarket
12. high school
13. drugstore
14. library

4

Word stress and vowel clarity

 ## A *Clear vowels*

Listen to this word. Which -a- has a clear vowel sound?

> ban **a** na

Only the stressed -a- is said with a clear sound. When a syllable is stressed, the vowel in it is extra clear as well as extra long.

B *Schwa*

The other two vowels in banana are *reduced* to a very short, unclear sound. This is the sound of the reduced vowel, *schwa*.

- There is no letter for this sound, but the dictionary symbol for schwa is /ə/.
- All of the vowel sounds in English can be reduced to schwa.
- Schwa is the most common vowel sound in English.

C *The contrast between schwa and clear vowels*

Listen. Notice the difference between schwa and the sound of a stressed vowel.

1. travel	tr**a**vəl		6. Kansas	K**a**nsəs
2. pilot	p**i**lət		7. Alaska	əl**a**skə
3. ticket	t**i**ckət		8. Nebraska	Nəbr**a**skə
4. pencil	p**e**ncəl		9. Canada	C**a**nədə
5. advice	ədv**i**ce		10. America	əm**e**rəcə

🎧 **D** | **Saying the contrast between schwa and clear vowels**

1 Listen. Underline the vowel in the stressed syllable of each word.

1. r<u>ea</u>søn
2. listen
3. excuse
4. allow
5. exchange
6. African
7. attend
8. arrange
9. record
10. American
11. Irish
12. pronounce
13. announce
14. Spanish

2 Draw a slash through the vowels that are reduced to a schwa sound.

3 Practice saying the words. Make the vowel in the stressed syllable long and very clear but the reduced vowels short and unclear.

E | **Pair work: Contrasting clear and reduced vowels**

Student A: Say one word from each pair of words.
Student B: Say the other word in the pair.

Take turns choosing a word to say first. Be careful to make the reduced vowels short and unclear.

Example

> Student A: "Atom."
> Student B: "Tom."

1. Tom	Tom	–	atom	atəm
2. face	face	–	surface	surfəce
3. at	at	–	attend	əttend
4. man	man	–	woman	womən
5. men	men	–	women	womən
6. office	offəce	–	official	əfficiəl
7. add	add	–	addition	əddition
8. added	addəd	–	additional	ədd%itiənəl

F Identifying and saying schwa

1 Listen. Draw a slash through the vowels that are reduced to schwa.

1 reduced vowel

probl~e~m
jacket
photograph
overcast
extra

2 reduced vowels

dr~a~mat~i~c
economics
adopted
application
collection

2 Practice saying the words.

G Vowel length and vowel clarity

In each word below there is one extra long, clear vowel and one vowel that is reduced to schwa. Each of these words also has one vowel that is not extra long, but is not reduced to schwa, either.

1 Listen.

concentrate   photograph   telephone

c**O**ncəntrate   ph**O**təgraph   tel**e**ləphone

2 Practice saying the words.

3 Read the rules below.

Stress Rules for Vowel Length and Vowel Clarity

1. The vowel in a stressed syllable is extra long and extra clear.

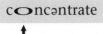
c**O**ncəntrate
↑

2. The vowel in an unstressed syllable is short and clear.

c**O**ncəntrate
↑

3. The vowel in a reduced syllable is very short and unclear (schwa).

c**O**ncəntrate
↑

Stressed vowels Long, clear	Unstressed vowels Short, clear	Reduced vowels Very short, very unclear
a e i o u	a e i o u	ə ə ə ə ə
Very easy to hear	Easy to hear	Hard to hear

H Identifying stress in multi-syllable words

1 Listen. Underline the stressed vowel in each word.

1. <u>a</u>ttitude	5. secondary	9. constitution
2. institute	6. reconsider	10. destination
3. gratitude	7. California	11. university
4. military	8. permission	12. understand

2 Practice saying the words.

I Limerick

1 Listen. The stressed vowels in this limerick are long and clear.
Most of the other vowels are reduced to schwa.

A **stu**dent was sent to Ta**co**ma
In**ten**ding to earn a di**plo**ma.
    He said, "With the **rain**,
    I don't want to re**main**.
I think I'd pre**fer** Okla**ho**ma."

2 Read the limerick out loud. Then whisper it, to help you
concentrate on the contrast between stressed and reduced vowels.

Note: Tacoma, Washington, is an especially rainy city, and
Oklahoma is an especially dry state.

J *The vowel sounds in "can" and "can't"*

Because it is important to make a contrast between "can" and "can't," in sentences, "can't" is usually said with the clear vowel sound /æ/, but the vowel sound in "can" is usually reduced to /ə/.

Listen to the following sentences. Notice the difference between the vowels in "can" and "can't."

We　cæn't　do it.

We　cən　do it.

They said they　cæn't　be there

They said they　cən　be there.

You　cæn't　have mine.

You　cən　have mine.

K *Pair work: "Can" and "can't"*

Student A: Say sentence **a** or **b**.
Student B: Say the matching response.

Take turns choosing a sentence to say. Do not always choose sentence **a**.

Example

> Student A: "I can't go."
> Student B: "That's too bad!"

1. a. I can go.　　　　　　Oh, good!
   b. I can't go.　　　　　That's too bad!

2. a. She can do it.　　　　That's wonderful.
   b. She can't do it.　　　She should try harder.

3. a. Where can we go?　　Any tourist destination.
   b. Where can't we go?　Into the military zone.

4. a. We can leave now.　　Good, I'll get my coat.
   b. We can't leave now.　All right, we'll wait.

5. a. Can you lift this?　　Of course.
   b. Can't you lift this?　No, I can't.

6. a. Why can you do that? Because I have permission.
   b. Why can't you do that? Because I don't know how.

7. a. What can we do? Make an effort.
   b. What can't we do? Fly without an airplane.

L Music of English 🎵

1 Listen to the following sentences.

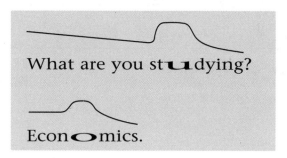

2 Listen again. Then practice saying the sentences until you can say them smoothly and easily.

M Check yourself: Stressed syllables

1 Listen to the dialogue. Circle the stressed syllable in the underlined words.

> *Students*
> A: What are you <u>studying</u>?
> B: <u>Economics</u>. What about you?
> A: <u>Photography</u>.
> B: Then you must take good <u>photographs</u>.
> A: And you must be good with <u>money</u>!

2 Practice saying the dialogue.

3 If you have a tape recorder, record the dialogue and listen to it. Did you make the stressed vowels extra long and extra clear?

VOWEL WORK

 N _The letters -y- and -w- as vowel sounds_

In many words, the letters -y- and -w- are pronounced as vowel sounds.

1 Sometimes the letter -y- sounds like the alphabet vowel sound /iʸ/ in "tea" or the alphabet vowel sound /aʸ/ in "ice."

Listen and repeat these words.

tea /iʸ/		ice /aʸ/	
funny	happy	why	apply
pretty	lazy	sky	type
city	comedy	my	reply
electricity	studying	fly	shy
history	photography	cry	supply

2 When the letter -y- follows the letter -a- in a word, it often acts like a second vowel. For words like this, the Two Vowel Rule usually works.

Listen and repeat these words.

cake /eʸ/	
say	today
pays	astray
stayed	dismay
may	player
way	always

3 When the letter -y- follows the letter -e- in the last syllable of a word, the Two Vowel Rule usually works.

Listen and repeat these words.

tea /iʸ/	
donkey	hockey
honey	monkeys
money	valley
alley	chimney

4 When the letter -**w**- follows the letter -**o**- in a word, it often acts like a second vowel. The Two Vowel Rule usually works for these words as well.

Listen and repeat these words.

| cone /oʷ/ |

show	knowing
slow	grows
blow	snow
throw	row
below	tow

5 Practice saying these sentences.

1. I want to apply for the job, but I can't type.
2. Give her the money so she can pay.
3. That was a very funny show.

🎧 ⓪ *Linking vowels with an off-glide* ⊂⊃⊂⊃⊂⊃⊂⊃⊂⊃

English speakers link words together in natural speech. The final sound in one word often connects with the first sound in the next word, with no pause between the words.

For example, when the words "we agree" are said together, it sounds like one word, "weagree."

When the vowel sounds /iʸ/, /aʸ/, or /eʸ/ link with a following vowel, the vowel sounds are connected by the off-glide / ʸ/.

1 Listen and notice how these words are linked by an off-glide.

1. We agree.   Weʸagree.
2. I often say a lot.   Iʸoften sayʸa lot.

2 Say these words together at least two times. Continue to say the final sound of the first word until you start to say the next word.

1. say it	sayʸit	4. pay us	payʸus
2. I am	Iʸam	5. cry out	cryʸout
3. stay away	stayʸaway	6. see everything	seeʸeverything

3 Say the following sentences, linking with the off-glide / ʸ/.

1. Primary education is very important.

2. We always try to see everything.

3. They all want to say it.

P Dictation

Listen and write down the sentences you hear.

1. My hobby is painting

2.

3.

4.

5.

5 Word stress patterns

A Listening to stress patterns

Every English word has a stress pattern. Using the correct pattern is even more important than using the correct sounds.

Listen to the following words and pay attention to the stress pattern.

☐☐☐
President

☐ ☐☐☐
Prime Minister

If you say words using their correct stress pattern, it is easier for other people to understand you, even if you do not get every sound exactly right.

B Review: Identifying stressed syllables

Listen. Underline the stressed syllable in each word. Remember that the vowel in the stressed syllable is extra long and extra clear.

<u>ham</u>burger	extremely	refrigerate	electric
cookies	accurate	refrigerator	electrical
pizza	dinner	refrigeration	electrification

C Stress in two-syllable words

1 Read this rule for predicting the stress pattern of two-syllable words.

Stress Rule for Two-Syllable Words

Except for verbs, two-syllable words are usually stressed on the first syllable.

---

2 Listen and repeat these two-syllable words.

□□ ▭□

lemon   **lᴇ**mən   rocket

jacket   **ja**ckət   open

older   **ᴏ**ldər   student

winter   April

3 Listen and repeat these two-syllable names.

Susan   **Su**sən   Richard

Allen   **A**llən   Kevin

Emma   **E**mmə   Michael

Lisa   Adam

Robert   Alice

4 Can you think of other two-syllable English names that have the same stress pattern?

D   *Stress in words that end in* -tion, -sion, *and* -cian

The following words all end in the letters **-tion**, **-sion**, or **-cian**. All of these endings are pronounced /ʃən/.

1 Listen to the stress pattern of these words. Underline the stressed syllable.

3 □□□	4 □□□□	5 □□□□□	6 □□□□□□
re<u>duc</u>tion	elec<u>tri</u>cian	participation	identification
musician	complication	examination	electrification
correction	occupation	administration	systematization
permission	politician	contamination	experimentation
instruction	regulation	verification	generalization

2 Say the words while paying attention to the stress pattern.

3 Can you figure out what the rule is for stress in words that end in **-tion**, **-sion**, or **-cian**?

> ### Stress Rule for the /ʃən/ Ending
>
> For words that end in **-tion**, **-sion**, or **-cian**, the stressed syllable comes just before the **-tion**, **-sion**, or **-cian** ending.

4 Use the rule above to find the stressed syllable in the words below. Underline the stressed syllable and then say the words.

pre<u>dic</u>tion	magician	education	commission
vacation	election	impression	aggravation

E Stress in words that end in -ic and -ical

1 Listen. Which syllable is stressed in the following words?

Atlantic	robotic	comic	terrific	automatic
electric	narcotic	economic	Pacific	photographic
domestic	statistic	dramatic	diplomatic	democratic

2 Write down what you think the stress rule is for words that end in **-ic**. Check your answer on the last page of this unit.

> ### Stress Rule for the -ic Ending
>
> ....
>
> ....

3 Listen. Which syllable is stressed in the following list of words?

economical
technological
surgical
comical
political
chemical

4 Write a rule for stress in these words. Check your answer on the last page of this unit.

Stress Rule for the -ical Ending

....

....

F Pronouncing two clear vowels together

When two vowels are next to each other in a word, but in separate syllables, they are both clear. Usually, the second clear vowel has the stress, so it is longer.

Listen and repeat these words.

biology   bi**o**logy   piano   pi**a**no   reaction   re**a**ction

reality   geography   geology
create   recreation   association

G Stress in two-syllable nouns and verbs

The following two-syllable words have a noun form and a verb form.

1 Listen and underline the stressed syllables. Which syllable is stressed for the nouns? Which syllable is stressed for the verbs?

Noun	Verb
1. <u>record</u>	re<u>cord</u>
2. object	object
3. permit	permit
4. suspect	suspect
5. import	import
6. rebel	rebel
7. present	present
8. conflict	conflict
9. insult	insult

2 Practice saying the noun and verb form of each word.

3 Read this rule.

> **Stress Rule for Two-Syllable Verb Forms**
>
> When a two-syllable word can be used as a noun or a verb, the verb form is usually stressed on the second syllable.

H *Which word do you hear?*

Listen. Circle the word you hear.

Noun	Verb
1. **con**tract	(con**tract**)
2. **ex**port	ex**port**
3. **prog**ress	pro**gress**
4. **re**ject	re**ject**
5. **trans**port	trans**port**
6. **pre**sent	pre**sent**
7. **con**flict	con**flict**
8. **con**vert	con**vert**

I *Stress in two-word verbs*

Some verbs are made up of two words. These two-word verbs are commonly stressed on the second syllable.

Listen to the stress pattern for these nouns and two-word verbs.

Noun	Verb
1. a **set**up (an arrangement)	set **up** (to arrange)
2. a **hold**up (a robbery)	hold **up** (to stop something)
3. a **look**out (a person who watches)	look **out** (to be careful)
4. a **try**out (a test, an audition)	try **out** (to test something or someone)
5. a **check**out (a place to pay a bill)	check **out** (to pay a bill and leave)
6. a **turn**off (something you do not like)	turn **off** (to displease)
7. a **cut**back (less of something)	cut **back** (to use less of something)

Music of English 🎵🎶

1 Listen to the following sentences.

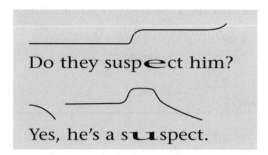

2 Listen again. Then say the sentences at least three times, until you can say them easily, like a little song.

K **Pair work: Noun or verb?**

Student A: Say the noun (**a**) or the verb (**b**) in the first column.
Student B: Say the sentence that contains the noun or verb that your partner said.

Take turns choosing words to say. Do not say the noun every time.

Examples

> Student A: "**Sus**pect."
> Student B: "He's a **sus**pect."
>
> Student A: "Ob**ject**."
> Student B: "We ob**ject** to that!"

1. a. **sus**pect   He's a **sus**pect.
   b. sus**pect**   Do they sus**pect** him of the crime?

2. a. **ob**ject   What's this little **ob**ject?
   b. ob**ject**   We ob**ject** to that!

3. a. **re**cord   Our team has the **re**cord for most wins.
   b. re**cord**   We re**cord** every victory.

4. a. **pre**sent   We gave her a **pre**sent.
   b. pre**sent**   They plan to pre**sent** her with an award.

5. a. **con**flict   It was a terrible **con**flict.
   b. con**flict**   His views con**flict** with mine.

6. a. **con**tract   They agreed to sign a **con**tract.
   b. con**tract**   Cold air makes metal con**tract**.

7. a. **check**out   We need to pay at the **check**out.
   b. check **out**   We need to check **out** of the hotel.

8. a. **cut**back   There might be a **cut**back in our pay.
   b. cut **back**   They may cut **back** on the number of workers.

9. a. **con**trast   There's a **con**trast between dark and light.
   b. con**trast**   The author wants to con**trast** good and evil.

L Stress in compound nouns

English often combines two nouns to make a new word, called a
compound noun. For example, the words "house" and "boat"
can be combined to form a new noun.

1 Listen.

> house + boat = **house**boat

Compound nouns are pronounced as a single word, with the stress
on the first part.

Note: Sometimes compound nouns are written as one word and
sometimes they are written as two words. Check your dictionary.

2 Practice saying these compound nouns.

houseboat	**shoe**box	**post** office
bathroom	**key**board	**disk** drive
raincoat	**note**book	**key** chain
passport	**bas**ketball	**light** bulb
bookstore	**base**ball	**cof**fee pot
dishwasher	**lunch**box	**speed** limit
airline	**book**mark	**phone** book

M Check yourself: Dialogue

1 Look at the underlined words in the following dialogue. The
stressed syllables are in bold.

2 Read the dialogue out loud, making the vowels in the stressed
syllables extra long and clear.

Note: For most people, "business" has two syllables. The letter -u-
in the first syllable has the relative vowel sound /ɪ/ as in "his."
For most people, "interesting" has three syllables.

Conversation on a Train

(Two commuters are talking while on their way to work in the city.)

First Commuter:	What **bus**iness are you in?
Second Commuter:	Pho**to**graphy.
First Commuter:	Oh yeah? **In**teresting. Is there a lot of **mon**ey in it?
Second Commuter:	Well, you have to look **out** for ex**pen**ses. They can cre**ate** a real **prob**lem.
First Commuter:	Really? And how much **mon**ey do you need to set **up** a **bus**iness like that?
Second Commuter:	Oh, a lot! The **set**up is ex**pen**sive – **chem**icals, photo**graph**ic e**quip**ment. Lots of stuff.
First Commuter:	I see. Well, maybe I'll just stick to my **pre**sent occu**pa**tion.

3 If you have a tape recorder, record yourself saying the dialogue. Did you lengthen the stressed syllables?

VOWEL WORK

  N | **The spelling -ow- pronounced /ɑʷ/ as in "cow"**

As you learned in Unit 4, the letters **-ow-** are usually pronounced with the sound /oʷ/, as in "know" and "show." But sometimes -ow- is pronounced with a different vowel sound, /ɑʷ/ as in "cow."

1 Listen and repeat these words.

cow /ɑʷ/	
now	brown
how	crowd
down	allow
town	towel
gown	powder

2 Practice saying these sentences.

1. This town is very crowded.
2. Please hand me the brown towel.
3. Now she understands how to do it.

O The spelling -ew- pronounced /uʷ/ as in "new"

Syllables spelled with **-ew-** are usually pronounced /**uʷ**/. This is the same sound as the vowel in "blue."

1 Listen and repeat these words.

> blue /**uʷ**/

knew	new
chew	crew
grew	few
stew	jewel
flew	sewage

2 Practice saying these sentences.

1. The baby is trying to chew with her new teeth.
2. The crew knew how to fly, but they refused.
3. Our puppy grew very fast in a few weeks.

P Linking vowels with an off-glide

When the vowel sounds /oʷ/, /ɑʷ/, or /uʷ/ link with a following vowel, the sounds are connected by the off-glide / ʷ/.

1 Listen and notice how these words are linked by an off-glide.

1. Please go on.   Please goʷon .

2. How about it?   Howʷabout it?

3. I knew it.   I knewʷit .

2 Say these words together at least two times. Continue to say the final sound of the first word until you start to say the next word.

1. new edition	new ᵂedition	5. how old	how ᵂold
2. a few eggs	few ᵂeggs	6. throw it	throw ᵂit
3. so often	so ᵂoften	7. no ice	no ᵂice
4. blue ocean	blue ᵂocean	8. go out	go ᵂout

3 Say these sentences, linking with the off-glide / ᵂ/.

1. I know all the songs, so I can lead the singing.
2. How old is the new edition?
3. We flew over the blue ocean.
4. There's no snow anywhere.

Q *Dictation*

Listen and write down the sentences you hear.

1. *He knows how to play the piano* ....
2. ....
3. ....
4. ....
5. ....

Answers to Task E (pages 36–37)

2 *Stress Rule for the* **-ic** *Ending:*
For words that end in **-ic**, the stressed syllable comes just before the **-ic** ending.

4 *Stress Rule for the* **-ical** *Ending:*
For words that end in **-ical**, the stressed syllable comes just before the **-ical** ending.

6 *Sentence focus: Emphasizing content words*

A *Emphasis in sentences*

Compare the two pictures below. In the picture on the left, the butterfly is hard to see because it is the same color as the things around it. The butterfly on the right is lighter than everything else around it. This contrast between light and dark emphasizes the butterfly and makes it easy to notice.

In a similar way, English speakers use contrast to emphasize the words they want their hearer to notice.

If you learn to use contrast to emphasize important words, you will:

- Be understood better.
- Hear better.

 ## B *Emphasizing a word*

1 Listen to these sentences and notice how the underlined words are easier to hear than the other words.

1. We'll be arriving <u>tomorrow</u>.
2. You look <u>great</u>.
3. She lives in <u>Toronto</u> now.
4. Is the baby <u>walking</u> yet?
5. Follow that <u>car</u>!

2 The underlined words in these sentences are easier to hear because they have been given extra emphasis. In English, extra emphasis is added to a word by:

- Making the vowel in the stressed syllable extra long and very clear.
- Adding a *pitch change* to the stressed syllable. This means making the pitch of your voice rise or fall on the stressed syllable.

3 Listen to the sentences again. Notice how each underlined word is emphasized.

C *Sentence focus*

In each short sentence or clause there is a *focus word*. The focus word is the most important word. English speakers help listeners notice the focus word by giving it the most emphasis.

"Car" is the focus word in the following sentence. It must be emphasized so that the hearer can notice it easily.

Follow that car!

Listen and notice how the stressed syllable of the focus word is extra long and clear and has a pitch change.

Follow that car !

Do you mean the blue one?

Focus Rule 1

The stressed syllable of a focus word is extra long, extra clear, and has a pitch change.

Music of English

1 Listen to these sentences and notice how the focus words are emphasized. The stressed syllable of each focus word has a change in pitch and a long, clear vowel.

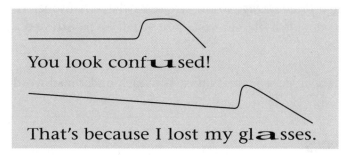

You look conf**u**sed!

That's because I lost my gl**a**sses.

2 Listen again. Practice saying the sentences until you can say them smoothly and easily.

E Focus and content words

Content words are words that carry the most information in a sentence. Nouns, main verbs, adverbs, adjectives, and question words are content words. Here are some examples from each category.

Nouns	Main verbs	Adverbs	Adjectives	Question words
cat	run	suddenly	fresh	who
bus	read	carefully	green	what
glasses	eat	slowly	confused	how

> **Focus Rule 2**
>
> The focus word in a sentence is usually a content word.

F Thinking of content words

Work in small groups. How many content words can you think of for each category?

Nouns	Main verbs	Adverbs	Adjectives	Question words

G Emphasizing the focus word

The focus words in these sentences are underlined. Each of these
focus words is a different category of content word.

1 Listen to the sentences and hear how the focus words are
emphasized.

1. My cat eats f**i**sh. (noun)

2. He l**o**ves it. (main verb)

3. But only fr**e**sh fish. (adjective)

4. He eats sl**o**wly. (adverb)

5. I don't know wh**y** he eats that way. (question word)

2 Practice saying the sentences.

H Adding the focus word

1 Add a content word to each sentence. The content word you
add will be the focus word.

1. I can't .... (main verb)
2. He's riding a .... (noun)
3. The baby is .... (main verb)
4. Please hand me the .... (noun)
5. The food is much too .... (adjective)
6. I'm not sure .... she's going. (question word)
7. He drives .... (adverb)

2 Practice saying the sentences. Emphasize the focus words.

Pair work: Dialogue

1 Listen to the dialogue. The underlined content word in each sentence is the focus word.

Note: There are two focus words in the last sentence because it has two clauses.

Lost Glasses

A: You look con**fused**.
B: That's because I lost my **gla**sses!
A: Where'd you **leave** them?
B: If I **knew** that, I could **find** them!

2 Practice saying the dialogue. Be sure to add a pitch change and extra length to the stressed syllable of each focus word.

VOWEL WORK

J Review: Linking vowels with off-glides

1 Some of the words in the following stories link together with an off-glide. Draw a small ʸ or a small ʷ between the words to show which off-glide links them together.

2 Read the stories out loud, linking with the appropriate off-glide.

At the Beach

Weʸoften go to the beach on the weekend. We‿always go by car, because it's fastest. My roommate will try‿anything. He loves to surf, but he‿isn't a great surfer. He‿always falls off the surfboard. "What's the‿answer?" he‿asked me. "I hate to say‿it, but I think you should find another sport," I said.

Jokes Between Friends

Sometimes I go ᵂover to my friend's house. The first thing she says when we meet is "How are you?" But if I really tell her how I am, she doesn't listen. This happens so often that I decided to answer "fine" every time.

But then one day I said, "You never listen." So she apologized and said, "From now on I'll do better." Then she asked, "How are you?" and I said "Terrible!" She knew I was joking, so she said, "That's great! See how I'm listening to everything you say?"

K Dictation

Listen and write down the sentences you hear.

1. *We all want the best solution*
2.
3.
4.
5.

7 Sentence focus: De-emphasizing structure words

A Focus and structure words

Most words that are not content words are **structure words**. Structure words are short words like "the" and "to" that don't carry as much information as content words. The focus word in a sentence is not usually a structure word.

Pronouns, prepositions, articles, "to be" verbs, conjunctions, and auxiliary verbs are structure words. Here are some examples from each category.

Pronouns	Prepositions	Articles	"to be" verbs	Conjunctions	Auxiliary verbs
she	of	a	is	and	can
him	to	an	was	but	have
ours	at	the	were	yet	do

> ### Focus Rule 3
> Structure words are usually de-emphasized to contrast with the focus word. This contrast makes it easier for the hearer to notice the focus word.

B Thinking of structure words

Divide into groups. Write as many structure words as you can think of for each category.

Pronouns	Prepositions	Articles*	"to be" verbs	Conjunctions	Auxiliary verbs
....	....	a	....	....	....
....	....	an	....	....	....
....	....	the	....	....	....
....	....		....	....	....
....	....		....	....	....

---

* These are the only articles in English.

There are different ways to de-emphasize a structure word in English. One way is by *contraction*.

"To contract" means to make smaller. Auxiliary verbs and the word "not" are normally contracted and connected to the word that comes before them. This helps to make these structure words less noticeable, and makes the more important words easier to notice.

1 Notice how the following structure words are contracted.

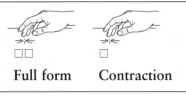

You + have	=	You've
He + would	=	He'd
Can + not	=	Can't
I + will	=	I'll

Note: You do not have to use contractions when you speak, but it is important for you to learn to hear them easily. That is why it is useful to practice them.

2 Listen to the difference between some common contractions and their full forms. Repeat the words and tap for each syllable.

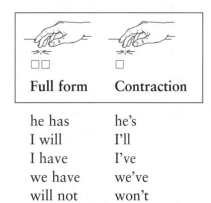

Full form	Contraction		Full form	Contraction
I am	I'm		he has	he's
do not	don't		I will	I'll
they have	they've		I have	I've
that is	that's		we have	we've
I would	I'd		will not	won't

D *Group work: Saying contractions*

Divide into two groups.

Group A: Say the first word of the full form.
Group B: Say the second word of the full form.
Both groups: Say the contraction together.

Example

Group A:	"She."
Group B:	"Is."
Both groups:	"She's."

	Full form	Contraction
1.	she is	she's
2.	can not	can't
3.	I have	I've
4.	why have	why've
5.	he has	he's
6.	who is	who's
7.	where did	where'd
8.	we are	we're
9.	they are	they're
10.	he had	he'd

E *Pair work: Saying contractions in sentences*

Student A: Say sentence **a** or **b** with the contraction.
Student B: Say the correct full form.

Take turns choosing a sentence to say. Do not always choose sentence **a**.

Example

Student A:	"They'd already gone."
Student B:	"They had."

	Contraction	Full form
1. a.	They've already gone.	they have
b.	They'd already gone.	they had
2. a.	Where'd you put that?	where did
b.	Where'll you put that?	where will

3. a. We're shut down completely.   we are
   b. We'd shut down completely.   we had

4. a. We'd be pleased to help.   we would
   b. We'll be pleased to help.   we will

5. a. They'll cut the bread.   they will
   b. They've cut the bread.   they have

6. a. What've you put in the soup?   what have
   b. What'll you put in the soup?   what will

7. a. Where'd everybody go?   where did
   b. Where'll everybody go?   where will

8. a. I've run in that race.   I have
   b. I'll run in that race.   I will

F   *Saying common expressions with contractions*

Listen and repeat these common friendly greetings and expressions. Each one contains a contraction.

1. What's new?
2. How're you doing?
3. How's it going?
4. How've you been?
5. What's up?
6. What'll you have? (to eat or drink)
7. It's great to see you!
8. I don't believe it!

G   *Linking in common expressions*

Some of the words in these common expressions link together. For example, the final /z/ sound in "how's" connects with the vowel sound in "it" so that the two words sound like one word, "howzit."

1 Listen and notice how some of the words in these expressions link together.

1. How's it going?   Howzit going?

2. What's up?   Whatsup ?

3. I don't believe it!   I don't believit !

2 Practice saying these expressions again.

H   De-emphasizing structure words: Reductions

Some structure words in English are de-emphasized by reducing the vowel in the structure word to schwa. Reducing structure words in this way makes the more important words easier to notice. Words that begin with a vowel sound, like "a," "an," and "or," are often linked to the final sound of the word that comes before them.

He takes a bus to work.   He takesə bus tə work.

1 Listen to the way the vowels in many of the structure words are reduced to schwa. Also notice how the structure words "a," "an," and "or" link to the word that comes before them.

1. He takes a bus to work.   He takesə bus tə work.

2. They wrote a letter to the president.   They wroteə letter tə thə president.

3. I left an umbrella in your car.   I leftən umbrella in yər car.

4. She runs or swims every day.   She runsər swims every day.

2 Practice saying the sentences.

Note: You do not have to use reductions in your speech. However, practicing reductions will help you to understand them in other people's speech.

I   De-emphasizing structure words: Reduced "and"

The structure word "and" is de-emphasized by reducing it to /ən/. The vowel sound is reduced to schwa, and the letter -d- is silent. The schwa sound in "and" is also linked to the final sound of the word that comes before it.

When "and" is reduced, the word before it and the word after it are easier to notice.

Cream and sugar   Creamən sugar

Listen to the way "and" is reduced and linked to the word that comes before it.

cream and sugar   creamən sugar

men and women   menən women

rock and roll   rockən roll

J Linking with reduced "and"

Practice saying these phrases with reduced "and." Remember to link the reduced "and" to the word that comes before it.

cats and dogs   knives and forks

sandwich and coffee   bread and butter

big and little   hamburgers and fries

rich and famous   salt and pepper

tables and chairs   boys and girls

K De-emphasizing structure words: Silent letter -h-

Pronouns like "he" and "her" that begin with the letter -h- are reduced by making the -h- silent. The vowel sound after the silent -h- links with the word that comes before it. For example, the question "Is he?" usually sounds like "Izzy?"

Is he?

1 Listen. Notice how the beginning -h- in each pronoun is silent. Also notice how the vowel in the pronoun links over the silent -h- to the word that comes before it.

1. What's her name?   Whatser name?

2. Call him.   Callim .

3. I can't reach her.   I can't reacher .

4. Matt lost his jacket.   Matt lostiz jacket.

5. Will he be there?

6. Has anyone seen him?

Note: When a pronoun beginning in -h- is the first word in a sentence, the -h- is not silent. For example, the -h- is not silent in the sentence "He's going."

2 Practice saying the sentences.

L Pair work: Linking over the silent letter -h-

1 Read the following sentences and draw an X through each -h- that should be silent.

2 Draw linking marks to connect the vowel after the silent -h- to the word that comes before it.

3 Student A: Say sentence **a** or **b**.
Student B: Say the matching response.

Take turns choosing a sentence to say. Do not always choose sentence **a**.

Example

> Student A: "Did he go?"
> Student B: "No, he didn't."

1. a. Did ̶he go?   No, ̶he didn't.
   b. Did she go?   Yes, she did.

2. a. Is her work good?   Yes, she does well.
   b. Is his work good?   Yes, he does a great job.

3. a. Give him a call.   I don't have his number.
   b. Give me a call.   Okay, what's your number?

4. a. Did you take her pen?   No, it's mine.
   b. Did you take your pen?   No, I forgot.

5. a. Is this his apartment?   No, he lives upstairs.
   b. Is this Sue's apartment? No, she lives downstairs.

6. a. Is he busy?   No, he isn't.
   b. Is she busy?   Yes, she is.

M Pair work: Dialogue

1 Read the dialogue that follows. Cross out each -h- that should be silent. (There are five.)

2 Listen to the dialogue to see if you crossed out every silent -h-.

The Missing Singer

Stage Manager: Where's our singer?
Assistant: I think he's practicing, sir.
Stage Manager: But we need him on stage now!
Assistant: Well, you know how nervous he gets.
Stage Manager: Did you tell him the concert's about to start?
Assistant: He's practicing just as fast as he can.

3 Practice the dialogue with a partner. Be sure to link over each silent -h-.

N Limerick

There are three pronouns with a silent -h- in the following limerick. Practice saying the limerick and be sure to link over each silent -h-.

A Train Ride

A singer once went to Vancouver,
Thinking the move would improve her.
    But the trip was so long,
    And her voice grew so strong,
At Toronto they had to remove her.

O Dictation

Listen and write down the sentences you hear.

1. *Did he give her the book?*
2.
3.
4.
5.

VOWEL WORK

P   The spelling -igh- pronounced /aʸ/ as in "night"

The spelling **-igh-** is pronounced /aʸ/. This is the same sound as the vowel in "ice."

1 Listen and repeat these words.

ice /aʸ/	
tight	sigh
night	high
sight	bright
right	tonight
thigh	mighty

2 Practice saying these sentences.

1. Make a right at the next light.
2. Tonight the sky will be bright with stars.
3. How high are we flying?

Q   The spelling -oo- pronounced /uʷ/ as in "moon"

The spelling **-oo-** is almost always pronounced /uʷ/. This is the same sound as the vowel in "blue."

1 Listen and repeat these words.

blue /uʷ/	
too	tool
noon	balloon
moon	foolish
cool	kangaroo
choose	boomerang

2 Practice saying these sentences.

1. Australia has kangaroos and boomerangs, too.
2. Which room did you choose?
3. I hope it's cooler this afternoon.

8 Choosing the focus word

A Focus at the beginning of a conversation

The following rule will help you to decide which word to emphasize when beginning a conversation.

> **Focus Rule 4**
>
> At the beginning of a conversation, the last content word in a clause or sentence is usually the focus word.

1 Listen to the following examples.

1. The dog chased a **ra**bbit.

2. We're w**ai**ting for you.

3. What are you d**o**ing?

2 Listen. Hum the melody of each sentence with the pitch pattern shown. (Humming is singing with your mouth closed.)

1. Here's a p**a**ckage for you.

2. Put this in the c**a**binet.

3. I lost my k**e**y.

4. I need some s**a**ndals.

3 Practice saying the sentences. Be sure to make the vowel in the stressed syllable of the focus word extra long and clear. Also be sure to change the pitch of your voice on the focus word.

B *Finding the focus word*

1 Underline the final content word in each of the following sentences. Circle the stressed syllable in this word.

1. There's no ele(ctri)city.

2. We need a photograph.

3. This is my sister.

4. Can I help you?

5. He doesn't understand it.

6. Where did you go?

7. Open the window for them.

8. Please record this for me.

2 Say the sentences with a pitch change on the stressed syllable. Also be sure to make the vowel in the stressed syllable extra long and clear.

C *Focus after the beginning of a conversation*

After a conversation begins, the focus changes because the speakers want to call attention to the *new thought* introduced in each new sentence. The focus word of the sentence that came before is now an *old thought*. It is already understood and does not need emphasis.

Focus Rule 5

After a conversation begins, the new thought in each sentence is the focus word.

---

1 Listen to this dialogue. Notice which word is the focus word in each sentence.

The Lost Hat

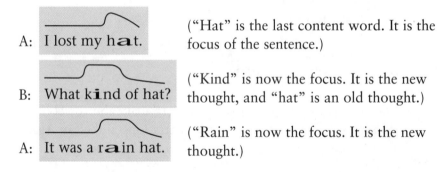

A: I lost my h**a**t.　("Hat" is the last content word. It is the focus of the sentence.)

B: What k**i**nd of hat?　("Kind" is now the focus. It is the new thought, and "hat" is an old thought.)

A: It was a r**a**in hat.　("Rain" is now the focus. It is the new thought.)

B: What c**o**lor rain hat?

A: It was wh**i**te. White pl**a**stic.

B: Hmmm. There was a white hat in the c**a**r.

A: Wh**i**ch car?

B: The one I s**o**ld!

2 Practice this dialogue with a partner. Be sure to emphasize the focus word in each sentence.

D *Pair work: Dialogues*

1 Listen and practice this dialogue. Use a change in pitch and an extra long vowel sound to emphasize the underlined focus words.

Child at the Shoe Store

Child: I want some **shoes**.

Parent: What **kind** of shoes?

Child: The **beau**tiful kind!

Parent: **Black** or **brown**?

Child: **Nei**ther. I'm **tired** of black and brown. I want **red** shoes. **Shi**ny red shoes!

Note: The fourth line above has two focus words, "black" and "brown." Both focus words are emphasized.

2 Underline the focus words in these dialogues. Some of the statements may have two focus words.

A Traveler

Travel Agent: Where do you want to go?

Traveler: China.

Travel Agent: Where in China? To the north or to the south?

Traveler: Neither. I've seen the north and south. I'm going east.

Two People on the Street

Woman: What are they building?
Man: They're building a school.
Woman: What kind of school? Elementary or high school?
Man: Neither. I think it's a trade school.

A Tourist

Tourist: What's the best part of Canada?
Canadian: That depends. Do you prefer the city or the countryside?
Tourist: Well, I like scenery.
Canadian: Then you should go to the far north of the country.
Tourist: Do they have good shopping there?
Canadian: Maybe you'd better go to Toronto.

Two Students

First Student: What are you doing?
Second Student: I'm studying.
First Student: Studying what? Math or English?
Second Student: Neither. I'm sick of math and English. I'm studying nutrition, because I'm always hungry.

3 Read the dialogues out loud and practice making the focus clear.

E   Music of English ♪♫

1 Listen to these sentences. Notice which words are the focus words.

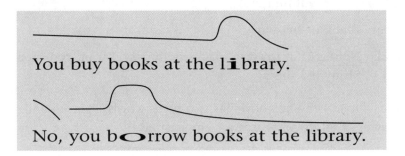

You buy books at the **li**brary.

No, you b●rrow books at the library.

2 Listen again. Practice saying the sentences until you can say them easily.

1 Listen. Notice how the focus word in the second sentence below ("month") is a correction for the word "week" in the first sentence.

> A: He was in Spain for a **week**.
> B: No, he was in Spain for a **month**.

2 Listen. In the second sentence below, the word "France" is a correction for the word "Spain" in the first sentence.

> A: He was in Spain for a **week**.
> B: No, he was in **France** for a week.

Focus Rule 6

When there is a disagreement or a correction, the word that corrects the information from the previous statement is the new focus word.

---

3 Practice saying these dialogues with a partner. Emphasize the underlined focus words. Take turns as Speaker A and Speaker B.

1. A: I buy books at the **li**brary.
   B: No, you **bo**rrow books at the library.

2. A: I buy books at the **li**brary.
   B: No, you buy books at the **book**store.

3. A: Madrid is the capital of **Ger**many.
   B: No, it's the capital of **Spain**.

4. A: Madrid is the capital of **Ger**many.
   B: No, Ber**lin** is the capital of Germany.

5. A: "Actual" means "in the present **time**."
   B: No, "actual" means "**real**."

6. A: A ship is smaller than a **boat**.
   B: I don't **think** so. A ship is **bigg**er than a boat.

7. A: Is Dallas in Cali**for**nia?
   B: No, it's in **Tex**as.

8. A: Is Dallas in Cali**for**nia?
   B: No, but San Fran**cis**co is in California.

G | Pair work: Listening for the focus word

Student A: Say sentence **a** or **b**.
Student B: Listen closely for the focus word, and say the matching response.

Example

> Student A: "It's a **big** dog."
> Student B: "No, it's really more **me**dium-sized."
>   OR
> Student A: "It's a big **dog**."
> Student B: "No, it's a **wolf**."

One way to make this exercise more fun is to hum the sentence.
Or you could use a kazoo (toy humming instrument). When
Student A hums the sentence, Student B listens closely to the pitch
pattern and then says the response.

1. a. It's a big **dog**.   No, it's a **wolf**.
   b. It's a **big** dog.   No, it's really more **me**dium-sized.

2. a. But we asked for two **cof**fees!   Oh, I thought you wanted **tea**.
   b. But we asked for **two** coffees!   Oh, I thought you wanted **one**.

3. a. I thought you bought a big **car**.   No, it was a **mo**torcycle.
   b. I thought you bought a **big** car.   No, it was a **litt**le one.

4. a. Is that a silver **watch**?   No, it's a **brace**let.
   b. Is that a **sil**ver watch?   No, it's **plat**inum.

5. a. I prefer beef **soup**.   Not **stew**?
   b. I prefer **beef** soup.   Not **chick**en?

6. a. Is there milk in the re**frig**erator? No, it's on the **table**.
   b. Is there **milk** in the refrigerator? No, but there's **juice**.

H | Pair work: Disagreement

1 Write an answer that disagrees with each of the following
statements. Different answers are possible.

2 Underline the word in your answer that disagrees with the
previous statement. This is the focus word of your answer.

1. A: Canada is far away.

   B: *No, it's near. OR It's not as far as England.*

2. A: Paris and London are countries.

   B: ....

3. A: May is the fourth month of the year.

   B: ....

4. A: It's not important to study hard at school.

   B: ....

5. A. China is a small country.

   B: ....

3 Practice saying the dialogues with a partner.

What was said before?

When you listen to a conversation, you may not hear what one of the speakers has just said. When this happens, listening closely to the emphasis in the other person's response can help you to guess what might have been said before.

In each of the dialogs below, read Speaker B's answer. The focus word of the answer is underlined.

Can you guess what Speaker A may have said to get an answer with this emphasis? Write your guess. Different answers may be possible.

1. A: *Today is Monday.*
   B: No, today is <u>Tuesday</u>.

2. A: ....
   B: No, the wedding is on the <u>fifth</u> of April.

3. A: ....
   B: I don't agree. We need <u>more</u> rain.

4. A: ....
   B: But we prefer to keep the window <u>open</u>.

5. A: ....
   B: <u>Blue</u> is the best color for a car.

6. A: ....
   B: No, I think it's on page <u>seven</u>.

J Pair work: A disagreement

Listen and underline the focus words. Then practice the dialogue with a partner.

Two Students Argue

A: I bought some books at the <u>library</u>.
B: They don't sell books at the library. They lend books there. They sell books at the bookstore. Didn't you know that?
A: On Tuesdays they sell books at the library. Surplus books.
B: Surplus?
A: Books they don't need. Extra ones.
B: I didn't know that.
A: There's a lot you don't know.

K Music of English ♫♪

1 Listen to these sentences.

2 Listen again. Practice the sentences until you can say them smoothly.

L Pair work: Using focus words to check information

Here are two useful ways to ask about something you did not understand or did not hear clearly. You can emphasize a question word, or you can repeat the word you are unsure of.

1 Listen and practice being Speaker A and Speaker B.

    1. A: They got here at one o'**clock**.
         B: <u>**When**</u> did they get here?

    2. A: The party is on the third of **May**.
         B: The <u>**third**</u>?

2 Practice saying these sentences.

1. A: My **mo**ther-in-law is coming.
   B: **Who** is coming?

2. A: We're going to Hong **Kong**.
   B: **Where** are you going?

3. A: The stock market is behaving e**rra**tically.
   B: The stock market is doing **what**?

4. A: All of this work will have to be finished by **Wednes**day.
   B: Finished by **when**?

5. A: We need twenty more **plates**.
   B: **Twen**ty?

6. A: We have to finish the work before **Tues**day.
   B: Be**fore** Tuesday?

7. A: I'll be **leav**ing tomorrow.
   B: To**morr**ow?

VOWEL WORK

  M _The vowel sound /ɔ/ as in "saw"_

The most common pronunciations for the letter -a- are the relative vowel sound /æ/ as in "pan" and the alphabet vowel sound /eʸ/ as in "cake." However, there is another common vowel sound for this letter, the sound /ɔ/ as in "saw."

Note: In Canadian English and in parts of the United States, /ɔ/ as in "saw" and /ɑ/ as in "top" are pronounced as the same sound. For example, some people pronounce "caught" and "cot" in the same way.

1 Listen to the sound /ɔ/ in words where the letter -a- is followed by -w-. Repeat each word after you hear it.

saw /ɔ/

paw	dawn
jaw	prawn
law	crawl
lawn	awful
fawn	lawful

2 Listen to /ɔ/ in these words where the letter -a- is followed by -u-. Repeat each word after you hear it.

| saw /ɔ/ |

cause   applaud
author   nautical
laundry   audible
caution   caught
saucer   taught

3 Listen and repeat these words where the letter -a- is followed by the letters -ll- or -lk-.

| saw /ɔ/ |

all   recall
fall   walk
ball   chalk
tall   talk
stall   stalk

4 Practice saying these sentences.

1. Who taught the baby to walk?
2. We all applauded the singers.
3. The word "nautical" means something about the sea.
4. We got up at dawn.

9 Emphasizing structure words

A Emphasizing structure words

As you learned in Unit 6, English speakers use contrast to emphasize the words they want their hearers to notice. The most important word, the focus word, is given the most emphasis so that it can be heard easily.

You also learned in Unit 6 that the focus word in a sentence is usually a content word and not a structure word. Structure words are de-emphasized to contrast with the words that are more important.

Sometimes, however, a structure word is the most important word in a sentence.

1 Listen to the following sentences. Speaker B is strongly disagreeing with Speaker A, so the structure word "am" is the most important word in Speaker B's sentence. Notice how it is emphasized.

A: You'll have to wait until you're **o**ld enough.

B: But I **a**m old enough!

2 Listen to these sentences. The structure word "and" is emphasized in Speaker B's statement because it corrects the word "or" in Speaker A's statement.

A: I think she's either sc**a**red or exc**i**ted.

B: Maybe she's scared **a**nd excited.

> **Focus Rule 7**
>
> When a speaker feels strongly or wants to correct something that was said before, a structure word may be emphasized.

B Music of English 🎵🎵

1 Listen to the music of these sentences. In the first sentence, the structure word "and" is reduced. In the response, "and" is the focus word, so it is emphasized.

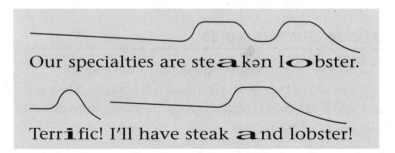

2 Listen again. Practice the sentences until you can say them smoothly.

C Pair work: Emphasizing "and" and "can"

"And" and the auxiliary verb "can" are usually reduced. But these structure words are emphasized when they are the focus word in a sentence.

Listen. Then practice saying these sentences with a partner. Emphasize the focus words with a pitch change and a long, clear vowel sound.

1. A: Our specialties are **steak** and **lob**ster.
   B: Ter**rif**ic! I'll have steak **and** lobster!

2. A: Which is more important – in**tell**igence or **eff**ort?
   B: **Both**. You need intelligence **and** effort.

3. A: Did you call at **eight** or at **nine**?
   B: I called at eight **and** at nine.

4. A: Do you think you can do the **job**?
   B: **Yes**, I **can**!

5. A: He can write **well**.
   B: Yes, he **can**, when he **wants** to.

D Pair work: Emphasizing auxiliary verbs

Usually, auxiliary verbs like "do," "be," and "have" are contracted. But when they are the most important word in a sentence, they are said in their full form.

Listen to each pair of sentences, and notice how auxiliary verbs are emphasized. Practice saying the sentences with a partner.

1. A: I don't have to **work** today.
   B: Yes, you **do** have to work, and right **now**.

2. A: That's a mean **dog**.
   B: Yes, it **is** a mean dog, but not as mean as **mine**.

3. A: You haven't stopped by in a long **time**.
   B: Yes, I **have** stopped by, but you're never **here**.

4. A: I don't think the train's **leav**ing.
   B: Sorry, but I see that it **is** leaving.

5. A: I'm not **go**ing.
   B: Yes, you **are** going!

6. A: He won't **pay** you.
   B: Well, I say he **will** pay me!

7. A: We're **rea**dy. Why aren't **you**?
   B: But I **am** ready.

8. A: Why don't you **like** it?
   B: But I **do** like it.

E Dialogue: Emphasizing "and" and auxiliary verbs

1 Read this dialogue and pay close attention to the emphasis in each sentence. In some of the sentences, structure words are emphasized.

A Short Commute
(Two coworkers are talking while at the office.)

A: [1]How do you get to **work** in the morning?
   Do you **walk** or ride the **bus**?
B: [3]I **walk** here. You should walk to work **too**.
   It's good **ex**ercise.
A: [5]As a matter of fact, I **do** walk to work.
B: But I've seen you on the **bus**!
A: [7]Maybe you **have**, but how do you suppose
   I **get** to the bus? I **walk**.
B: [9]Oh, so you walk **and** ride the bus.
A: Ex**act**ly.

2 Practice the conversation with a partner.

3 With your partner, discuss why you think structure words are emphasized in lines 5, 7, and 9. Check your answers on the last page of this unit.

F Pair work: Emphasizing prepositions and pronouns

Prepositions like "in" and "on" and pronouns like "I" and "they" can be the focus word in a sentence when they correct or contrast with a word that was said before.

Notice how prepositions and pronouns are emphasized in the responses below. Practice saying the sentences with a partner.

1. A: Is the cat on the **bed** again?
   B: No, she's **un**der the bed.

2. A: You forgot to leave the keys on the **desk**.
   B: I'm **sorr**y. I put them **in** the desk.

3. A: If you're going **out**, please buy some **butt**er.
   B: Sorry, I'm just now coming **in**.

4. A: I'm **freez**ing.
   B: It doesn't seem cold to **me**.

5. A: Did you misplace the **keys**?
   B: No, **you** were the one who had them last.

6. A: Do you like to argue with your **friends**?
   B: No, but they like to argue with **me**.

7. A: **Hi**! What's **new**?
   B: Nothing **much**. What's new with **you**?

G Pair work: Emphasizing pronouns that begin with -h-

You learned in Unit 7 that when a pronoun begins with the letter -h-, the -h- is often silent. But when the pronoun is the focus word, the -h- is pronounced.

Take turns being Speaker A and Speaker B. Be sure to emphasize the focus words.

1. A: Does she like classical **mus**ic?
   B: No, but **he** does.

2. A: Where's Michael's **En**glish book?
   B: **I** don't know. Ask **him** about it.

3. A: Jerry showed me your fine re**port**.
   B: It's not **mine**. It's mostly **his** work.

H *Emphasizing pronouns*

1 Listen to this poem. Do you understand why the underlined pronouns are emphasized? Check your answer on the last page of this unit.

> ¹Behold the hippopotamus!
>   We laugh at how he looks to us,
> ³And yet in moments dark and grim
>   I wonder how <u>we</u> look to <u>him</u>.
> ⁵Peace, peace, thou hippopotamus!
>   We really look all right to us,
> ⁷As <u>you</u> no doubt delight the eye
>   Of other hippopotami.
>
> – Ogden Nash

2 Practice saying the poem.

I *Dialogue: Emphasizing focus words*

1 Read the following dialogue. Can you explain why the speaker emphasizes structure words in lines 3, 5, and 10? The answers are on the last page of this unit.

Strange Diet

A: ¹Do you think food in this country is ex**pen**sive?
B: No, not **real**ly.
A: ³Well, **I** think it's expensive.
B: That's because you eat in **rest**aurants.
A: ⁵Where do **you** eat?
B: At **home**.
A: ⁷Do you know how to **cook**?
B: No, I just eat **bread** and **tea**.
A: ⁹That isn't **sen**sible!
B: Yes it **is** sensible. I **like** bread and tea.
A: ¹¹You're **crazy**!

2 Practice the dialogue with a partner.

3 If you have a tape recorder, record yourself saying the dialogue. Then listen to check if you emphasized the focus words.

J Review: The Focus Rules

Here is a list of the focus rules you learned in Units 6 through 9.

Focus Rule 1
The stressed syllable of a focus word is extra long, extra clear, and has a pitch change.

Focus Rule 2
The focus word in a sentence is usually a content word.

Focus Rule 3
Structure words are usually de-emphasized to contrast with the focus word. This contrast makes it easier for the hearer to notice the focus word.

Focus Rule 4
At the beginning of a conversation, the last content word in a clause or sentence is usually the focus word.

Focus Rule 5
After a conversation begins, the new thought in each sentence is the focus word.

Focus Rule 6
When there is a disagreement or a correction, the word that corrects the information from the previous statement is the new focus word.

Focus Rule 7
When a speaker feels strongly or wants to correct something that was said before, a structure word may be emphasized.

VOWEL WORK

  K   Different vowel sounds for the letter -a-

You have learned three vowel sounds for the letter -a-. These sounds are /eʸ/ as in "cake," /æ/ as in "pan," and /ɔ/ as in "saw."

Listen and circle the word you hear.

cake /eʸ/	pan /æ/	saw /ɔ/
1. paid	pad	(pawed)
2. pain	pan	pawn
3. pained	panned	pawned
4. take	tack	talk
5. bake	back	balk
6. stake	stack	stalk
7. Kate	cat	caught

L ___The contrast between /ɔ/ and /ɑ/___

Listen and circle the word you hear.

Note: In Canadian English and parts of the United States, /ɔ/ and /ɑ/ are pronounced as the same sound, so words like "caught" and "cot" sound the same.

saw /ɔ/	top /ɑ/

1. stalk   (stock)
2. dawn   Don
3. caught   cot
4. pawed   pod
5. pawned   pond

 M ___Saying the contrast between /ɔ/ and /ɑ/___

Listen and repeat these sentences.

1. Don't talk back to a cop.
2. I heard the alarm clock at dawn.
3. A baby deer is a fawn.
4. Someone who watches sports is a fan.
5. I saw him stocking boxes in the back.

10 Continuants and stops: /s/ and /t/

A _Introducing continuants and stops_

1 Look at the parts of the mouth in this picture.

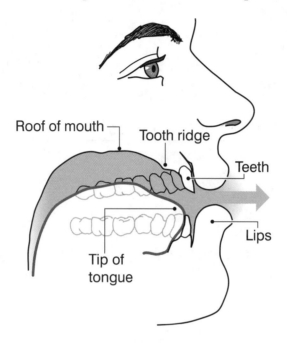

Different speech sounds are made by the way air flows out over the tongue. When the tongue touches different parts of the mouth, the air flow changes, which changes the sound you hear.

2 For many sounds we let the air flow through the mouth without stopping it. These sounds are called *continuants*.

Listen to the following word and notice how the final sound continues.

bussss

3 In other sounds, we stop the air flow inside the mouth. These sounds are called *stops*.

Listen to this word and notice how the final sound stops.

but

4 Look at pictures of these two sounds, /**s**/ and /**t**/, seen from different directions.

bus /s/   but /t/

Looking from the side

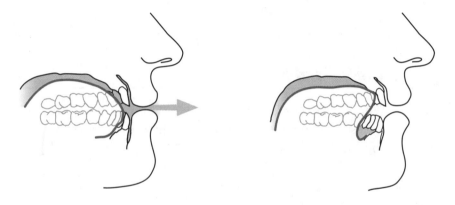

Looking to the front

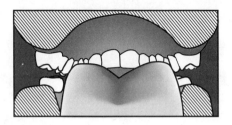 

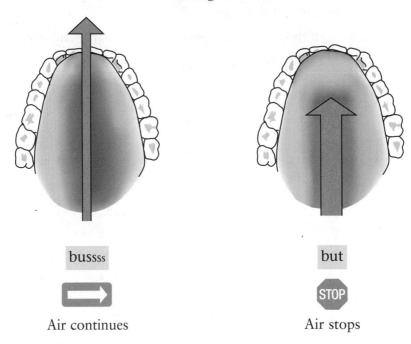

Looking down

bussss

Air continues

but

STOP

Air stops

B *Saying* /s/ *and* /t/

1 Whisper the words "bus" and "but," and feel the difference
between the final /s/ sound and the final /t/ sound. During /s/,
you can feel the air flow out. For /t/, the air is stopped.

2 Practice saying these words out loud.

bus, but, bus, but

C *Which word is different?*

Listen. Mark the column for the word that is different.

	X	Y	Z	
1.	....	....	✔	(lice, lice, light)
2.	....	....	....	
3.	....	....	....	
4.	....	....	....	
5.	....	....	....	
6.	....	....	....	
7.	....	....	....	
8.	....	....	....	

D Which word do you hear?

1 Listen. Circle the word you hear.

Note: Sometimes the letter **-c-** is pronounced /**s**/ as in "race" and "rice."

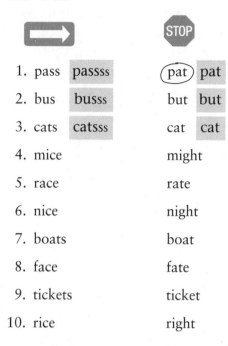

	→		STOP	
1.	pass	passss	(pat)	pat
2.	bus	busss	but	but
3.	cats	catsss	cat	cat
4.	mice		might	
5.	race		rate	
6.	nice		night	
7.	boats		boat	
8.	face		fate	
9.	tickets		ticket	
10.	rice		right	

2 Practice saying the words you circled.

E Music of English ♫♪

1 Listen to the following questions. Notice that the focus words are emphasized by a pitch change and a long, clear vowel in the stressed syllable.

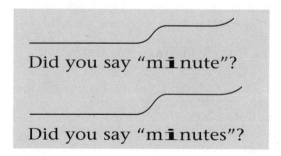

Did you say "m**i**nute"?

Did you say "m**i**nutes"?

2 Listen again. Practice saying the questions until you can say them smoothly.

F   *Pair work: Singular and plural words*

The continuant sound /**s**/ is often used at the end of a word to make it plural.

Student A: Say a word from each pair of words.
Student B: If the word is singular hold up one finger. If the word is plural hold up all five fingers.

Take turns choosing a word to say.

Examples

Student A: "Minutes" Student B: (Hold up five fingers.)	
Student A: "Night." Student B: (Hold up one finger.)	

1. minutes   minute
2. nights   night
3. lights   light
4. tickets   ticket
5. jackets   jacket
6. seats   seat
7. mats   mat
8. boats   boat

G   *Pair work: Is it singular or plural?*

Student A: Say sentence **a** or **b**.
Student B: Say "singular" or "plural."

Take turns saying sentences. Do not always choose sentence **a**.

Examples

Student A: "Read your books." Student B: "Plural."

1. a. Read your book.
   b. Read your books.

2. a. Bring your map tomorrow.
   b. Bring your maps tomorrow.

3. a. Copy your report every day.
   b. Copy your reports every day.

4. a. I put the ticket in my pocket.
   b. I put the tickets in my pocket.

5. a. Where did you put the cake?
   b. Where did you put the cakes?

6. a. Did you enjoy your trip?
   b. Did you enjoy your trips?

7. a. Please clean the mat now.
   b. Please clean the mats now.

8. a. Fill the bucket with hot water.
   b. Fill the buckets with hot water.

H Pair work: Saying sentences with /s/ and /t/

Student A: Ask question **a** or **b**.
Student B: Say the matching answer.

Example

Student A: "How do you spell 'night'?" Student B: "N - I - G - H - T."

1. a. How do you spell "night"?   N - I - G - H - T.
   b. How do you spell "nice"?   N - I - C - E.

2. a. How do you spell "bought"?   B - O - U - G - H - T.
   b. How do you spell "boss"?   B - O - S - S.

3. a. What does "mice" mean?   The plural of "mouse."
   b. What does "might" mean?   "Power."

4. a. Do you have the tickets?   They're in my pocket.
   b. Do you have the ticket?   It's in my pocket.

5. a. How do you spell "right"?   R - I - G - H - T.
   b. How do you spell "rice"?   R - I - C - E.

6. a. What does "less" mean?   The opposite of "more."
   b. What does "let" mean?   To allow.

7. a. Did you buy the coats?   Yes, one for each of us.
   b. Did you buy the coat?   Yes, I'm wearing it.

8. a. Did you say "minute"?   No, I said "second."
   b. Did you say "minutes"?   Yes, ten minutes.

Linking with /s/

When a word ends in the continuant sound /s/, the final /s/ links to a vowel at the beginning of the next word. There is no pause between the two words.

less of   lessssof

1 Listen and repeat these words. Link the final /s/ to the vowel at the beginning of the next word.

less of	pass it	Miss Anderson
lessssof	passssit	MissssAnderson

chase after   let's agree   nice evening

2 Practice linking with /s/ in the following sentences.

1. The boats entered the water.   boatsssentered
2. The coats all need to be cleaned.   coatsssall
3. She has less of everything.   lessssof
4. Is the boss in the office?   bossssin
5. The nights are long here.   nightsssare

Linking with /t/

When a word ends in the stop sound /t/, the final /t/ links to a vowel at the beginning of the next word.

get in   getin

1 Listen and repeat these linked words. Notice that when /t/ links with a vowel, it is said quickly.

get in	right answer	great ending
getin	rightanswer	greatending

bought everything   shout it   plate of

2 Practice linking with /t/ in the following sentences.

1. The boat entered the water.   boatentered
2. We need a lot of money.   lotof
3. It's right around the corner.   rightaround
4. We bought everything we could carry.   boughteverything
5. The bucket is empty.   bucketis

K Dictation

Listen and write down the sentences you hear.

1. *The tickets are in his pocket* ....

2. ....

3. ....

4. ....

5. ....

VOWEL WORK

L Practicing vowels with /s/ and /t/

1 Listen and circle the word you hear.

Words ending in /t/

1. ate	(at)	ought
2. bait	bat	bought
3. Kate	cat	caught
4. rate	rat	right
5. mate	meet	might

Words ending in /s/

6. base	bass	boss
7. mace	mass	mice
8. lace	lease	lice
9. moose	mouse	moss
10. pace	pass	peace

2 Practice saying the words you circled.

11 Continuants and stops: /r/ and /d/, /l/ and /d/

A Continuants and stops: /r/ and /d/

The /r/ sound is a continuant. When making this sound, the air flows out along the middle of the tongue without stopping.

1 Listen to this word and pay close attention to the final /r/ sound.

2 Listen to this word and pay attention to the final sound. It is the stop /d/.

3 The pictures on the left show the continuant sound /r/. Compare these with the pictures for the stop sound /d/ on the right.

near /r/   need /d/

Looking from the side

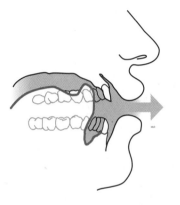   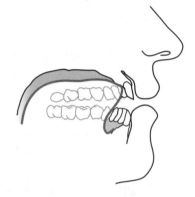

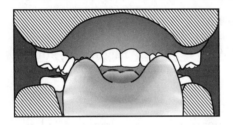

Looking down

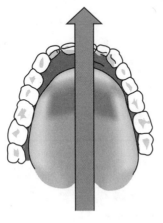
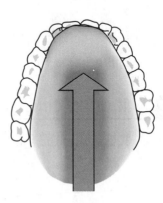

nearrrr

need

STOP

Air continues   Air stops

B *Saying* /r/ *and* /d/

1 *Silently* do this:
  • Raise your tongue so that you feel the sides of the tongue touch the upper tooth ridge toward the back of your mouth.
  • Do not let the tip of your tongue touch the roof of your mouth.

This is the position for the continuant sound /**r**/.

2 *Silently* raise your whole tongue so that you are pressing the tooth ridge all around and the air cannot flow out. This is the position for the stop sound /**d**/.

3 Practice whispering both these words. Then say them out loud several times.

hire, hide, hire, hide

C Which word do you hear?

1 Listen. Circle the word you hear.

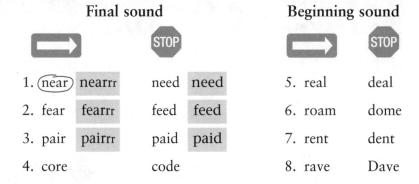

	Final sound				Beginning sound	
1.	(near) nearrr	need	need	5.	real	deal
2.	fear fearrr	feed	feed	6.	roam	dome
3.	pair pairrr	paid	paid	7.	rent	dent
4.	core	code		8.	rave	Dave

2 Practice saying the words you circled.

D Music of English ♫♪

1 Listen to the following sentences.

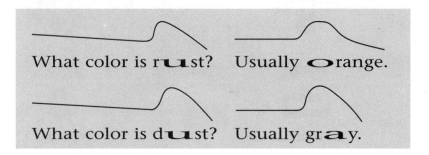

What color is r**u**st?   Usually **o**range.

What color is d**u**st?   Usually gr**a**y.

2 Listen again. Say the sentences until you can say them smoothly.

E Pair work: Saying sentences with /r/ and /d/

Student A: Ask question **a** or **b**.
Student B: Say the answer that matches the question.

Take turns asking questions. Do not always choose to say question **a**.

Example

> Student A: "What color is dust?"
> Student B: "Usually gray."

1. a. What color is rust?   Usually orange.
   b. What color is dust?   Usually gray.

2. a. How do you spell "rare"? R - A - R - E.
   b. How do you spell "dare"? D - A - R - E.

3. a. What's a dam? A wall for water.
   b. What's a ram? A male sheep.

4. a. What does "fear" mean? Feeling scared.
   b. What does "feed" mean? To give food.

5. a. What's the definition of "liar"? A person who tells lies.
   b. What's the definition of "dire"? Extremely serious.

6. a. What does "we're" mean? "We are."
   b. What does "weed" mean? A plant nobody wants.

7. a. Did he explode? Yes, he was furious!
   b. Did he explore? Yes, he went everywhere in the city.

8. a. What's the definition of "lie"? The opposite of "truth."
   b. What's the definition of "die"? To stop living.

F Linking with /r/

When a word ends in the continuant sound /r/, the final /r/ links to a vowel sound at the beginning of the next word.

hear us   hearrrus

Note: Many English words end in a silent letter -e-. Linking sounds go right over the silent -e-. For example, "where are" sounds like wherrrare .

1 Listen and repeat these linked words.

hear us	pair of shoes	her arm
hearrrus	pairrrof shoes	herrrarm

better offer   cure it   prepare everything

2 Read the following sentences and draw linking marks connecting words that end in /r/ to words that begin with a vowel sound.

1. Did you hear us?
2. There isn't a better answer.
3. I need a pair of shoes.
4. Do you want to share everything?
5. We're all here in the car.

3 Practice saying the sentences, being sure to link with the /r/ sound.

G *Linking with* /d/

When a word ends in the stop sound /**d**/, the final /**d**/ links to a vowel at the beginning of the next word. This makes it sound as if the final /**d**/ is the beginning of the next word. For example, "paid Ann" sounds like "pay Dan."

paid Ann   paidAnn

had it   hadit

1 Listen and repeat these linked words.

paid Ann	I had it	answered everyone
paidAnn	I hadit	answeredeveryone

told us   good answer   mad at me

2 Read the following sentences and draw linking marks connecting words that end in /**d**/ to words that begin with a vowel sound.

1. I had it this morning.
2. She said everything.
3. You told us last week.
4. The parade always starts early.
5. I did only the first part.
6. She had always wanted us to sing.
7. They answered every question.
8. Her grade is perfect.

3 Practice saying the sentences, being sure to link with the /**d**/ sound.

H *The sound combination* /r/ **+** /d/

1 Listen and circle the word you hear.

1. car   carrr   (card)   card
2. her   herrr   heard   heard
3. share   shared
4. prepare   prepared
5. hire   hired
6. retire   retired
7. bore   bored
8. care   cared

2 Practice saying the words you circled.

I Pair work: Past or present?

A final /d/ sound is often used to make a verb past tense.

Student A: Say sentence **a** or **b**.
Student B: Say "past" or "present."

Take turns choosing a sentence to say. Do not always choose sentence **a**.

Example

> Student A: "We shared all the food."
> Student B: "Past."

1. a. We share all the food.
   b. We shared all the food.

2. a. The dogs scare every cat.
   b. The dogs scared every cat.

3. a. Some speakers bore us.
   b. Some speakers bored us.

4. a. They hire new employees on Friday.
   b. They hired new employees on Friday.

5. a. They fear every animal.
   b. They feared every animal.

6. a. The children share all the cookies.
   b. The children shared all the cookies.

7. a. We admire all your work.
   b. We admired all your work.

8. a. They pour milk into the glass.
   b. They poured milk into the glass.

J Continuants and stops: /l/ and /d/

1 The sound /l/ is another continuant sound. Listen to the word "bell," and pay close attention to the /l/ sound at the end of the word.

belllll

2 Compare these pictures of the continuant sound /**l**/ and the stop sound /**d**/.

bell /**l**/   bed /**d**/

Looking from the side

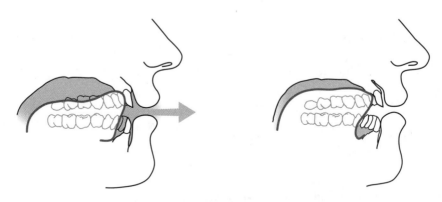

Looking to the front

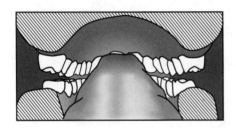   

Looking down

belllll   bed

Air continues   Air stops

3 *Silently* make an /l/ sound this way: Keep the tip of your tongue pressed against the tooth ridge at the front of your mouth, but lower the rest of the tongue. This allows the air to flow over the tongue and out on both sides of the raised tip. If you breathe in strongly through your mouth, you will feel the cold air coming back in over the sides of the tongue.

4 Practice the position for the /**d**/ sound again.

5 Experiment by whispering the words "bell, bed, bell, bed" several times. Then practice saying the words out loud.

K   *Which word do you hear?*

Listen. Circle the word you hear.

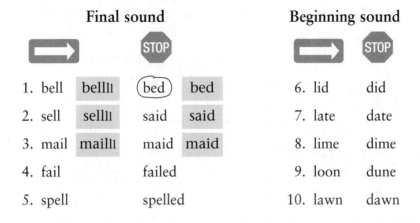

	Final sound				Beginning sound	
1. bell	bellll	(bed)	bed	6. lid	did
2. sell	sellll	said	said	7. late	date
3. mail	mailll	maid	maid	8. lime	dime
4. fail		failed		9. loon	dune
5. spell		spelled		10. lawn	dawn

L   *Pair work: Saying words with /l/ and /d/*

Student A: Say a word from each pair of words.
Student B: Say the other word in the pair.

Example

> Student A: "Wide."
> Student B: "While."

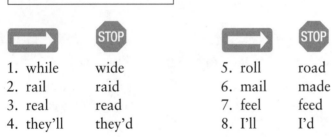

	STOP		STOP
1. while	wide	5. roll	road
2. rail	raid	6. mail	made
3. real	read	7. feel	feed
4. they'll	they'd	8. I'll	I'd

M   *Pair work: Saying sentences with final /l/ and /d/*

Student A: Say question **a** or **b**.
Student B: Say the matching answer.

Example

> Student A: "How do you spell 'kneel'?"
> Student B: "K - N - E - E - L."

1. a. How do you spell "need"?   N - E - E - D.
   b. How do you spell "kneel"?   K - N - E - E - L.

2. a. What does "they'll" mean?   "They will."
   b. What does "they'd" mean?   "They would" or "they had."

3. a. What does "rule" mean?   To govern.
   b. What does "rude" mean?   Not polite.

4. a. What does "fell" mean?   The past of "fall."
   b. What does "fed" mean?   The past of "feed."

5. a. What's the opposite of "well"?   "Sick."
   b. What's the opposite of "wed"?   "Unmarried."

6. a. How do you spell "seal"?   S - E - A - L.
   b. How do you spell "seed"?   S - E - E - D.

7. a. Why did she feed it?   It was hungry.
   b. Why did she feel it?   To see if it was hot.

8. a. What does "I'll" mean?   "I will."
   b. What does "I'd" mean?   "I had."

N   *Linking with /l/*

Words that end with the continuant sound /l/ link with words that begin with a vowel. For example, when the words "all eyes" are said together, it sounds like "all lies."

1 Listen and repeat these linked words.

sell everything	feel excited	I'll always
selleverything	feellexcited	I'lllalways

| roll over | call Allen | well enough |

2 Read the following sentences and draw linking marks connecting words that end in /l/ to words that begin with a vowel sound.

1. We want to sell everything.
2. Please tell us the news.
3. Are you well enough to work?
4. We have to pull up all the flowers before it snows.
5. I'll always call Allen on his birthday.

3 Practice saying the sentences. Be sure to link the /l/ at the end of a word to the vowel at the beginning of the next word.

Contractions with final /l/ and /d/

The auxiliary verbs "will," "would," and "did" are usually contracted in spoken English. For this reason, it is important for you to be able to hear the /l/ or /d/ sound at the end of words.

I would eat. ⟶ I'd eat.
I will eat. ⟶ I'll eat.

Listen. You will hear either sentence **a** or **b**. Circle the full form of the contraction you hear.

	Contraction	Full Form
1. a.	They'll ask a good question.	(They will)
b.	They'd ask a good question.	They would
2. a.	He'll answer soon.	He will
b.	He'd answer soon.	He would
3. a.	Do you think they'll like it?	They will
b.	Do you think they'd like it?	They would
4. a.	I said I'll do the work.	I will
b.	I said I'd do the work.	I would
5. a.	Who'll they ask?	Who will
b.	Who'd they ask?	Who did
6. a.	Where'll Ann find one?	Where will
b.	Where'd Ann find one?	Where did

P The sound combination /l/ + /d/

Listen and repeat the words below, concentrating on the combination of sounds at the end of each word.

filled	told
sold	spelled
failed	smiled
called	sailed

Q Music of English ♫♪

1 Listen to the following sentences.

Note: The first -c- in "succeed" is pronounced with the stop sound /**k**/. The second -c- in "succeed" is pronounced with the continuant sound /**s**/.

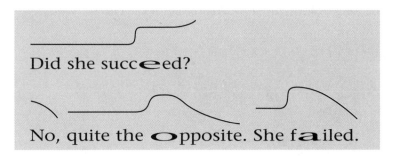

Did she succeed?

No, quite the opposite. She failed.

2 Listen again. Practice the sentences until you can say them smoothly. Be sure to emphasize the focus words.

R Pair work: Past or present?

Student A: Say sentence **a** or **b**.
Student B: Say "past" or "present."

Pay close attention to the final sound of the verb.

Example

> Student A: "We failed every time."
> Student B: "Present."

1. a. We fail every time.
   b. We failed every time.

2. a. They close everything.
   b. They closed everything.

3. a. I call you every night.
   b. I called you every night.

4. a. They usually stay late.
   b. They usually stayed late.

5. a. They arrive at six o'clock.
   b. They arrived at six o'clock.

6. a. We save all your letters.
   b. We saved all your letters.

7. a. Everything bored us.
   b. Everything bores us.

8. a. The children spill their juice.
   b. The children spilled their juice.

VOWEL WORK

S ### Using the Vowel Rules with /r/, /d/, and /l/

Use the One Vowel Rule and the Two Vowel Rule to decide how these words are pronounced. Practice saying each word.

Beginning /r/, /d/ and /l/

rake	rack	dine	din	lied	lid
ripe	rip	dame	dam	lease	less
reed	red	dime	dim	like	lick
ride	rid	duel	dull	laid	lad

Final /d/ and /l/

fade	fad	pile	pill
died	did	seal	sell
code	cod	mule	mull
bleed	bled	feel	fell
node	nod	pale	pal

T *Practicing vowels with /r/, /d/ and /l/*

1 Listen and circle the word you hear.

Words ending in /r/

1. fear   fair   (fire)
2. pure   pair   peer
3. hear   hair   hire
4. cure   core   care
5. dear   dare   dire

Words ending in /d/

6. seed   side   sad
7. feed   fade   fad
8. rude   rode   rod
9. reed   raid   ride
10. deed   died   did

Words ending in /l/

11. feel   fail   file
12. pal   pale   pill
13. peel   pill   pile
14. meal   mill   mile
15. rail   role   rule

2 Practice saying the words you circled.

12 Voicing

A Introducing voicing

1 Listen to the words "hiss" and "buzz."

This is the sound a snake makes:

hiss   hissss

This is the sound a bee makes:

buzz   buzzzz

2 Press your fingers against the opening of your ears, and say the word "hiss," continuing the final /s/ sound until you hear it clearly.

3 Press your fingers against the opening of your ears and say the word "buzz," continuing the final /z/ sound until you hear the difference from the /s/ sound.

The buzzing of the /z/ sound is called *voicing*. /z/ is a voiced sound. /s/ is a voiceless sound.

Note: When you whisper, you are not voicing any sounds.

4 Practice saying each sound, switching back and forth until you can hear the difference between the voiced and voiceless sounds.

/s/	/z/	/s/	/z/
Ssss	zzzz	Ssss	zzzz

B Which word is different?

Listen. Mark the column for the word that is different.

	X	Y	Z	
1.	....	....	✔	(eyes, eyes, ice)
2.	....	....	....	
3.	....	....	....	
4.	....	....	....	
5.	....	....	....	
6.	....	....	....	
7.	....	....	....	
8.	....	....	....	

C Saying words with /s/ and /z/

Listen and repeat each pair of words.

Note: The letter **-s-** is sometimes pronounced **/z/** as in "eyes" and "his."

Voiceless sound /s/   *Voiced sound* /z/

Beginning sound

sip	sip	zip	zip
sink	sink	zinc	zinc
Sue		zoo	
seal		zeal	

Final sound

bus	bus	buzz	buzz
fuss	fuss	fuzz	fuzz
place		plays	
miss		Ms.	

Middle sound

fussy	fussy	fuzzy	fuzzy
busing	busing	buzzing	buzzing
racing		raising	
facing		phasing	

98 • Unit 12

D Linking with /s/ and /z/

1 Practice saying these sentences. Link words that end in /s/ and /z/ to words that begin with a vowel sound.

Linking with /s/

1. Snakes hiss out of fear.　　　Snakes ⬚hissssout⬚ of fear.

2. Billy left a mess in the sink.　　Billy left a ⬚messssin⬚ the sink.

3. How nice of you to come!

4. Would you like a piece of pie?

Linking with /z/

5. His aunt called.　　　　　Hi⬚zzz⬚aunt called.

6. Has everybody left?　　　　Ha⬚zzz⬚everybody left?

7. My eyes are tired.

8. Where's Anne?

E Saying phrases with /s/ and /z/

Listen and repeat each word or phrase.

Voiceless sound /s/
1. hissing sound
2. snake
3. a sand snake
4. That's harmless.

Voiced sound /z/
5. buzzing noise
6. bees in the desert
7. amazing
8. Amazing, isn't it?

Voiceless sound /s/ and voiced sound /z/

9. sounds like bees　　　⬚soundz⬚ like ⬚beez⬚

10. hissing noise　　　　hissing ⬚noize⬚

11. That's amazing.　　　That's ⬚amazing⬚.

12. A poisonous snake?　　A ⬚poizonous⬚ snake?

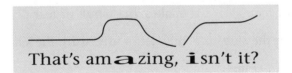

F Music of English ♪♫♪

1 Listen. This sentence has two focus words.

Note: The letter -s- in "that's" is voiceless and the letter -s- in "isn't" is voiced.

That's am**a**zing, **i**sn't it?

2 Listen again. Practice saying the sentence until you can say it smoothly. Be sure to make the vowel sound in the stressed syllable of each focus word long and clear.

G Pair work: Dialogue

Practice this conversation with a partner.

In the Desert

A: What's that buzzing noise?
B: It sounds like bees.
A: That's amazing, isn't it?
B: Not really. There are flowers and
   bees in the desert.
A: What's that hissing sound?
B: Sounds like a snake.
A: A snake! A poisonous snake?
B: No, it's a sand snake. They're harmless.

H The sounds /f/ and /v/

1 Listen to the sound /f/ in "leaf" and the sound /v/ in "leave."

leaf   leaf

leave   leave

2 Look at this picture of the mouth position for the sounds /**f**/ and /**v**/. The position is the same for the two sounds, but /**f**/ is voiceless and /**v**/ voiced.

Looking from the side
/**f**/ and /**v**/

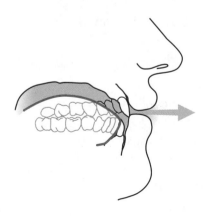

Saying words with /**f**/ and /**v**/

Listen and repeat the following pairs of words.

Voiceless sound /**f**/		*Voiced sound* /**v**/	
Final sound			
leaf	leaf	leave	leave
half	half	have	have
safe	safe	save	save
Beginning sound			
fat	fat	vat	vat
fine	fine	vine	vine
fault	fault	vault	vault

J   *Pair work: Saying words with /f/ and /v/*

Student A: Say a word from each pair of words.
Student B: Say "voiced" or "voiceless."
Student A: If the answer is wrong, repeat the word so your partner
can try again.

Take turns choosing a word to say.

Example

Student A:	"Van."
Student B:	"Voiceless."
Student A:	"No. Van."
Student B:	"Oh, it's voiced."

Beginning sound

Voiceless	Voiced
1. fan	van
2. fine	vine
3. fail	veil
4. fast	vast
5. ferry	very

Final sound

Voiceless	Voiced
6. leaf	leave
7. safe	save
8. half	have
9. proof	prove
10. belief	believe

Middle sound

Voiceless	Voiced
11. leafing	leaving
12. surface	service
13. rifle	rival
14. reference	reverence

K *Pair work: Asking questions with /f/ and /v/*

Student A: Ask question **a** or **b**.
Student B: Say the matching answer.
Student A: If the answer is wrong, repeat the question.

Examples

> Student A: "What does 'vine' mean?"
> Student B: "A kind of plant."
>
> Student A: "What does 'veil' mean?"
> Student B: "The opposite of 'succeed.'"
> Student A: "No. What does 'veil' mean?"
> Student B: "A covering for the face."

1. a. What does "fine" mean?   Something like "good."
   b. What does "vine" mean?   A kind of plant.

2. a. What does "veil" mean?   A covering for the face.
   b. What does "fail" mean?   The opposite of "succeed."

3. a. How do you spell "have"?   H - A - V - E.
   b. How do you spell "half"?   H - A - L - F.

4. a. What's a "v"?   A letter of the alphabet.
   b. What's a "fee"?   Cost for a service.

5. a. How do you spell "believe"?   B - E - L - I - E - V - E.
   b. How do you spell "belief"?   B - E - L - I - E - F.

6. a. What does "fear" mean?   To be afraid.
   b. What does "veer" mean?   To change direction fast.

7. a. Do you have a view?   Yes, I can see the lake.
   b. Do you have a few?   No, I don't have any.

8. a. What's a "volley"?   A shot in tennis.
   b. What's a "folly"?   A foolish act.

L *Voiced and voiceless sounds for the spelling -th-*

The letter combination **-th-** can be voiced or voiceless. Listen.

teeth	teeth	teethe	tee*the*
bath	bath	bathe	ba*the*

Note: The vowel sounds in "bath" and "bathe" are not the same.

The symbol for the voiceless **-th-** sound is /θ/, and the symbol for the voiced **-th-** sound is /ð/.

M *Voiceless -th-*

Listen and repeat these words. In all of these words, the letters **-th-** are pronounced with the voiceless sound /θ/.

Final sound	*Beginning sound*
teeth	thing
path	thought
math	thief
tooth	thunder

N *Voiced -th-*

1 Listen to the words below. Circle the words with a voiced /ð/ sound for the letters **-th-**.

1. (bathe)
2. breath
3. breathe
4. bath
5. math
6. they
7. think
8. thigh
9. those
10. this

2 Practice saying the words above.

O Linking with /f/, /v/, and the -th- sounds

Practice saying these sentences. Be sure to link final voiced and voiceless consonants to the vowels that come next.

Note: The spelling **-gh-** is often pronounced /**f**/ as in "laugh."

Voiceless final sounds

1. They laugh a lot.
2. Both are ready.
3. It's half empty.

4. Take a bath in hot water.
5. Read the fourth unit.
6. We know enough about it.

Voiced final sounds

7. Have a seat.
8. Save all your money.
9. Prove it.

10. Don't give up.
11. Breathe in slowly.
12. Bathe in cold water.

P Linking continuants

You have already learned that final voiced and voiceless continuants like /z/, /s/, /v/, /f/, /ð/, and /θ/ link with vowel sounds. Continuant sounds also link with other continuants.

1 Listen and repeat these words. Do not pause between the linked sounds.

his face	bus ride	half moon
hi**zzz**face	bus**ss**ride	half**fff**moon

| believe me | bathe slowly | math student |

2 Practice saying these sentences. Be sure not to pause between the linked continuant sounds.

1. His money's not here.   Hi**zzz**money**zzz**not here.

2. What's my grade?   What's**ss**my grade?

3. Let me know if Lisa calls.   Let me know if**ff**Lisa calls.

4. Excuse me.

5. I save letters.

6. We went with Sue.

7. Does she always laugh so loudly?

Q Review: Voiced and voiceless sounds for -th-

1 Listen to this limerick. Circle the words that begin with -th-.

> The teachers are quick to suggest
> That we study quite hard for a test.
>   It takes lots of thought
>   To learn what we're taught,
> So I think I'd prefer just to rest.

2 Read the limerick aloud several times. The sound of -th- in "the" and "that" should be the voiced sound /ð/. The sound of -th- in "thought" and "think" should be the voiceless sound /θ/.

R Pair work: Nouns and verbs

Student A: Say a noun or verb from each pair of words below.
Student B: Say "noun" or "verb."

Take turns choosing a word to say.

Examples

> Student A: "Prove."
> Student B: "Verb."
>
> Student A: "Teeth."
> Student B: "Noun."

Note: These verbs end with a voiced sound, and the nouns end with a voiceless sound.

Verbs		Nouns		Verbs		Nouns	
prove	prove	proof	proof	relieve	relieve	relief	relief
teethe	teethe	teeth	teeth	believe	believe	belief	belief
save		safe		devise		device	
grieve		grief		advise		advice	
use		use		excuse		excuse	

Pair work: Review of contractions with /v/, /d/, and /l/

Student A: Say sentence **a**, **b**, or **c**.
Student B: Say the full form of the contraction.

Take turns saying the sentences.

Example

> Student A: "They'd gone."
> Student B: "They had."

Contraction	Full form
1. a. They've gone.	they have
b. They'd gone.	they had
2. a. We'd eaten.	we had
b. We've eaten.	we have
3. a. Where'd you put it?	where did
b. Where'll you put it?	where will
c. Where've you put it?	where have
4. a. We'll come.	we will
b. We'd come.	we had
c. We've come.	we have
5. a. How've you come here?	how have
b. How'd you come here?	how did
c. How'll you come here?	how will
6. a. We'll shut the door.	we will
b. We'd shut the door.	we had
c. We've shut the door.	we have
7. a. They've put it away.	they have
b. They'll put it away.	they will
c. They'd put it away.	they had
8. a. Why'll you come?	why will
b. Why'd you come?	why did
c. Why've you come?	why have

Listen and write down the sentences you hear.

1. _Fall leaves are bright red_ ....

2. ....

3. ....

4. ....

5. ....

VOWEL WORK

🎧 **U** | **_The vowel sound /ɔʸ/ as in "boy" and "coin"_**

In stressed syllables, the spelling -oy- is always pronounced with the sound /ɔʸ/ as in "boy." The spelling -oi- is also often pronounced /ɔʸ/ as in "coin."

1 Listen and repeat these words with -oy- pronounced /ɔʸ/.

boy /ɔʸ/

joy	enjoy
boy	royal
toys	voyage
annoys	enjoyment
destroy	employment

2 Listen and repeat these words with -oi- pronounced /ɔʸ/.

boy /ɔʸ/

coin	point
join	poison
noise	ointment
voice	avoid
choice	disappoint

3 Practice saying these sentences.

1. The king is enjoying his royal voyage.
2. She found employment selling noisy toys.
3. You can avoid disappointment by joining our team.

13 Voicing and syllable length

🎧 **A** _**Introducing voicing and syllable length**_

The final sound of an English word is important because it may be a grammar signal. For example, the final consonant in a word may tell you if the word is a noun or a verb.

Final consonants are sometimes hard to hear, but there is an extra signal to help the listener know if the final consonant in a word is voiced or voiceless.

1 Listen to the words "save" and "safe." "Save" ends in a voiced consonant, and "safe" ends in a voiceless consonant.

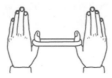

2 Listen to the words again. Pay attention to the vowel sound in each word. The vowel sound in "save" is longer than the vowel in "safe."

> **_Rule for Voicing and Syllable Length_**
>
> A vowel before a voiced consonant is longer than a vowel before a voiceless consonant.

B   Which word is different?

Listen. Mark the column for the word that is different.

1. ....   ✔   (save, save, safe)
2. ....
3. ....
4. ....
5. ....
6. ....
7. ....
8. ....

C   Pair work: Final voiced and voiceless continuants

Student A: Say a word from each pair below.
Student B: Say the other word in the pair.

Take turns choosing a word to say. If you choose a word that
ends in a voiced continuant, be sure to make the vowel extra long.

Example

> Student A: "Save."
> Student B: "Safe."

   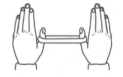

Voiceless continuant			Voiced continuant	
safe	safe	–	save	s**a**ve
cease	cease	–	seize	s**ei**ze
fuss	fuss	–	fuzz	f**u**zz
leaf	leaf	–	leave	l**ea**ve
bus		–	buzz	
race		–	raise	
half		–	have	
Miss		–	Ms.	
price		–	prize	

D Final voiced and voiceless stops

It is often difficult to hear final stop sounds in the speech of North Americans from the United States and Canada. For this reason, it is particularly important to notice the length of the vowel sound before the final stop. A lengthened vowel means that the final stop is voiced.

Practice saying these pairs of words. Be sure to lengthen the vowel before a final voiced stop.

Voiceless stop /t/		Voiced stop /d/	Voiceless stop /k/		Voiced stop /g/
bet	–	bed	back	–	bag
sat	–	sad	rack	–	rag
debt	–	dead	duck	–	dug
right	–	ride	pick	–	pig

Voiceless stop /p/		Voiced stop /b/
cap	–	cab
rope	–	robe
lap	–	lab
mop	–	mob

E Pair work: Final voiced and voiceless consonants in sentences

Student A: Say sentence **a** or **b**. Add length to the vowel if you choose the sentence with a voiced final consonant.
Student B: Say the matching answer.

Take turns choosing a sentence to say. Do not always choose sentence **a**.

Example

> Student A: "He wants peas."
> Student B: "Not carrots?"

1. a. He wants peas.   Not carrots?
   b. He wants peace.   Not war?

2. a. There's something in my eyes!   Call a doctor!
   b. There's something in my ice!   Call a waiter.

3. a. Is it in the bag?   No, in the box.
   b. Is it in the back?   No, in the front.

4. a. Isn't this a good prize?	Yes, did you win it?
b. Isn't this a good price?	Yes, it's really cheap.
5. a. What kind of word is "prove"?	It's a verb.
b. What kind of word is "proof"?	It's a noun.
6. a. What's a buck?	A dollar.
b. What a bug?	An insect.
7. a. What does "Miss" mean?	An unmarried woman.
b. What does "Ms." mean?	A woman.
8. a. What does "wrote" mean?	The past tense of "write."
b. What does "rode" mean?	The past tense of "ride."
9. a. What's a rope for?	To tie something up.
b. What's a robe for?	To keep you warm.

F Noun or verb?

In the lists below, the verbs end with voiced consonants and the nouns end with voiceless consonants. Therefore, the verbs have a longer vowel before the final consonant.

1 Listen. Circle the noun or verb you hear.

Verbs	Nouns		Verbs	Nouns
1. (prove) /v/	proof /f/	6. believe /v/	belief /f/
2. save /v/	safe /f/	7. devise /z/	device /s/
3. teethe /ð/	teeth /θ/	8. relieve /v/	relief /f/
4. excuse /z/	excuse /s/	9. grieve /v/	grief /f/
5. use /z/	use /s/	10. advise /z/	advice /s/

2 Practice saying the words you circled.

G Pair work: Which sentence contains the word?

Student A: Say the underlined word from sentence **a** or **b**.
Student B: Say the sentence that contains that word.

Example

> Student A: "Proof"
> Student B: "Bring proof tomorrow."

1. a. Can you <u>prove</u> it?
   b. Bring <u>proof</u> tomorrow.

2. a. Good <u>advice</u> is worth more than gold.
   b. I <u>advise</u> you not to go.

3. a. How long does a baby <u>teethe</u>?
   b. How many <u>teeth</u> does your baby have?

4. a. I <u>believe</u> you.
   b. "<u>Belief</u>" means "faith."

5. a. What <u>excuse</u> did they give?
   b. <u>Excuse</u> me.

6. a. I want to <u>save</u> money.
   b. Did you put your money in the <u>safe</u>?

7. a. This medicine should <u>relieve</u> the pain.
   b. It was a <u>relief</u> to me.

8. a. They never <u>use</u> the back door.
   b. The back door gets very little <u>use</u>.

H Pair work: Dialogue with voiced sound /z/ and voiceless sound /s/

1 Practice saying these phrases. Be careful to make the vowels before final voiced consonants extra long.

Voiced sound /z/

Excuse me.	Exc**u**ze me.
my eyes	my **e**yez
Close your eyes.	Cl**o**ze your **e**yez.
Is that wise?	**I**z that w**i**ze?
Is it dust?	**I**z it dust?

Voiceless sound /s/

It's sauce.	It's sause.
It's no use.	It's no use.
Place some ice on them.	Plase some ise on them.
Yes.	Yes.

Voiced sound /z/ and Voiceless sound /s/

Use the ice from this glass.   **U**ze the ise from this glass.

2 Practice this dialogue with a partner.

Trouble at the Restaurant

Customer: Excuse me, waiter!
Waiter: Yes? What's the matter?
Customer: There's something in my eyes.
Waiter: Is it dust?
Customer: No, it's sauce!
Waiter: It's no use rubbing them. Close your eyes and place some ice on them.
Customer: Is that wise?
Waiter: Yes! Use the ice from this glass.

Pair work: Dialogue

Listen to this dialogue. Then practice it with a partner.

Where's the Zoo?

Tourist: Could you please tell me how to get to the zoo from here?
Local: Sure. Just go straight up Lack Street until you get to Gray's Alley.
Tourist: Did you say "Grace"?
Local: No, no. Gray's. Then turn left on Gray's, and go another two or three blocks, and you'll be right in front of the main entrance.
Tourist: I appreciate the help. Thanks.
Local: No problem. Enjoy the zoo.

Pair work: Map game

1 Practice the street names on the map on page 116.

Student A: Say the name of a street on the map.
Student B: Point to that street.

2 Take turns saying these sample directions to your partner.

1. From here, go two blocks north on Pace Drive.
2. Turn east when you get to Leaf Avenue.
3. Go straight down Lag Drive until you get to White Avenue. Then turn right.
4. It's on the left-hand side.
5. It's opposite the entrance to Oakley Park.
6. Did you say "White" or "Wide"?

3 To play the game:

Each partner must have a copy of the map. One partner will be the "tourist" and the other partner will be the "local." The tourist wants to see all the important buildings in town.

1. Local: Look at your map and decide where you would like to place the first three buildings that are listed. Write the numbers of those buildings in the locations you choose.
2. Tourist: Look at your map and ask the local how to get to the first building on the list.
3. Local: Give clear directions to the building starting from the arrow marked "START HERE." Don't use your hands to show the tourist where the building is.
4. Tourist: Use your finger or a pencil to follow the directions on your map. Mark the spot where you think the building is located.
5. Local: Check to see if the tourist found the right building.
6. After three buildings, change roles. The new local now chooses where to put three more buildings, and the new tourist now asks for directions.

Example

Tourist:	"Can you please tell me how to get to the Oakley Mall?"
Local:	"Sure. Go two blocks north on Wide Avenue, and turn left on Leaf."
Tourist:	"Did you say, 'Leave'?"
Local:	"No, Leaf. After you turn left on Leaf, go west until you reach Lag Drive. Oakley Mall will be on your right."
Tourist:	(Mark the building that you found.)

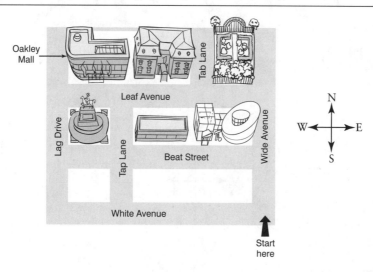

List of Buildings

1. Oakley Mall
2. Historical Society
3. Jazz Museum
4. Fine Arts Museum
5. Observation Tower
6. Hotel Oakley
7. Founder's Monument
8. Hall of Justice
9. Discount Delight Mall
10. Zoo
11. Botanical Gardens
12. Newspaper Office

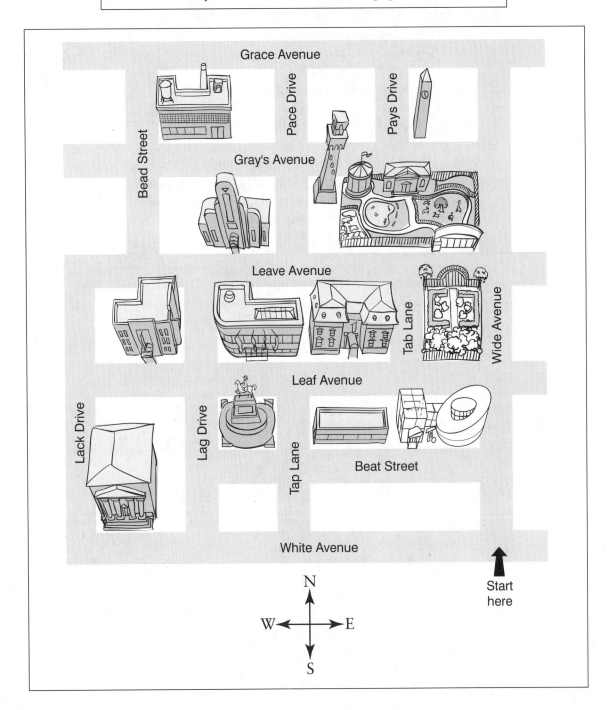

K Check yourself: Dialogue

Read the following dialogue from Task H again. If you have a tape recorder, record the dialogue by yourself or with a partner. Listen to the recording. Did you lengthen the vowels before voiced consonants?

Trouble at the Restaurant

Customer: Excuse me, waiter!
Waiter: Yes? What's the matter?
Customer: There's something in my eyes.
Waiter: Is it dust?
Customer: No, it's sauce!
Waiter: It's no use rubbing them. Close your eyes and place some ice on them.
Customer: Is that wise?
Waiter: Yes! Use the ice from this glass.

L Dictation

Listen and write down the sentences you hear.

1. *What kind of seat is this?*
2.
3.
4.
5.

M Review: Linking

Practice linking in these sentences. Say each sentence several times until the combination of the last two words sounds like a new word.

1. We don't fear ice.   rice
2. Where does the trail end?   lend
3. Please use ink.   zinc
4. Can we save Anne?   van
5. What is there to laugh at?   fat

VOWEL WORK

 N ___The spelling -ou- pronounced /aʷ/ as in "house"___

The letters **-ou-** are often pronounced /aʷ/. This is the same sound as the vowel in "cow."

1 Listen and repeat these words.

cow /aʷ/

house	proud
loud	sound
out	about
south	around
mouth	aloud

2 Practice saying these sentences.

1. They found a house.
2. What's that loud sound?
3. She went outside and walked around the block.

14 *Sibilants*

A *Introducing sibilants*

Sibilants are consonant sounds that make a hiss. This hissing sound comes from air rushing through a narrow valley along the speaker's tongue.

1 Listen to the following words. Each one ends in a different sibilant. Notice how the sibilants make a hissing sound.

Voiced sibilants	his /**z**/	beige /**ʒ**/	badge /**dʒ**/
Voiceless sibilants	hiss /**s**/	wash /**ʃ**/	batch /**tʃ**/

2 Look at the pictures below.

/**s**/ and /**z**/   /**ʃ**/ and /**ʒ**/

Looking from the side

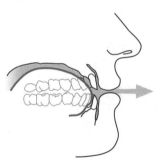 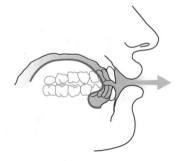

Looking down

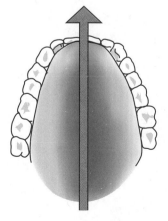 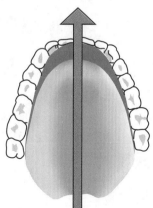

B Saying sibilants

1 To say /s/, press the sides of your tongue against your teeth so that a valley is formed down the center of your tongue. If you blow strongly, the air will rush through this narrow valley and make a high-pitched hissing noise as it goes past your front teeth. `Ssss`

The /ʃ/ sound is a little different. After whispering /s/ several times, move your tongue back just a little. Now there is more room for air to get out. With this position, the hissing noise will rush through the narrow valley with a lower pitch.

Make the /s/ and the /ʃ/ sounds several times, at first quietly, then aloud. If you blow out strongly, the sound for /s/ will be a higher hiss, and the sound for /ʃ/ will be a lower hiss. If you round your lips for /ʃ/, the difference between the two sounds will be more obvious.

2 Try both of these sounds with voicing. The sounds will now become /z/ and /ʒ/.

C Contrasting voiceless sibilants /s/ and /ʃ/

Listen and repeat these pairs of words.

Beginning sounds		Final sounds	
/s/	/ʃ/	/s/	/ʃ/
Sue	shoe	mass	mash
see	she	gas	gash
same	shame	mess	mesh
so	show	lease	leash

D Contrasting voiced sibilants /z/ and /ʒ/

Listen and repeat these pairs of words.

Middle sounds	
/z/	/ʒ/
laser	leisure
closing	closure
pleaser	pleasure
Caesar	seizure

E — Linking with voiceless sibilant /ʃ/

1 Practice saying the following words, linking the /ʃ/ sound to the vowel that comes next.

trash everywhere	crush it	cash only
trasheverywhere	crushit	cashonly

| fish all day | rush of water | push us |

2 Practice linking in these sentences.

1. A gash is a deep cut.
2. There was a flash of lightning.
3. Crush all the trash into the can.
4. Dogs must be on a leash at all times.

F — Contrasting /s/ (sick) and /θ/ (thick)

The voiceless -th- sound /θ/ is not a sibilant because the tongue is flat and relaxed, so there is no hissing sound. The /s/ sound makes a hiss because the air is forced through a narrow valley.

1 Look at these pictures.

sick /s/   thick /θ/

Looking from the side

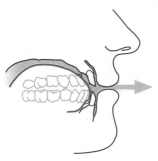
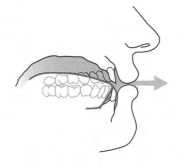

Looking to the front

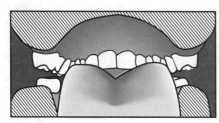
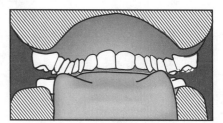

2 Listen and repeat these pairs of words.

Voiceless beginning sounds		Voiceless final sounds	
/θ/	/s/	/θ/	/s/
think	sink	math	mass
thank	sank	faith	face
thick	sick	myth	miss
thought	sought	mouth	mouse

G *Tongue twisters with* /s/, /ʃ/, *and* /θ/

Practice saying these tongue twisters.

/ʃ/ /z/   /ʃ/   /s/   /ʃ/
1. She is certain to show you the sailors from the ship.

/ʃ/ /s/   /s/ /ʃ/   /s/ /ʃ/
2. She sells seashells by the seashore.

/s/   /θ//s/   /s/   /s/   /θ/
3. Miss Beth Smith saw a mouse in the path.

H *Contrasting* /ʃ/ *(ship) and* /tʃ/ *(chip)*

The sibilant /tʃ/, as in "chip," is pronounced as a combination of the stop sound /t/, followed by the continuant sound /ʃ/.

1 Look at these pictures.

ship /ʃ/   chip /tʃ/

Looking from the side

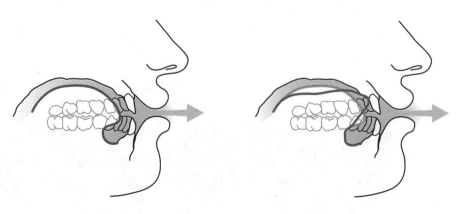

2 Listen and repeat these pairs of words.

Beginning sounds		Final sounds	
/ʃ/	/tʃ/	/ʃ/	/tʃ/
share	chair	wish	witch
shoe	chew	dish	ditch
sheep	cheap	mush	much
shop	chop	cash	catch

Contrasting /dʒ/ (jet) and /y/ (yet)

The sibilant /dʒ/, as in "jet," is pronounced as a combination of the stop /d/, followed by the continuant /ʒ/. The positions for /dʒ/ are the same as for /tʃ/ as in "chip," but with voicing. The sound /y/, as in "yes," is not a sibilant.

1 Listen and repeat these words beginning with the /dʒ/ sound.

Joe	joy	just	juice
jar	jury	job	jump
judge	jam	Jack	jewel

2 Listen and repeat these words beginning with the /y/ sound.

yes	young	year	yard
you	your	yet	yellow
yell	yesterday	you'll	yoke

3 Say these pairs of words.

/dʒ/	/y/
Jell-O®	yellow
jell	yell
joke	yoke
jet	yet
jail	Yale
jewel	you'll

J *Pair work: Contrasting /ʃ/, /tʃ/, /dʒ/, and /y/ in sentences*

Student A: Say sentence **a** or **b**.
Student B: Say the matching response.

Take turns choosing a sentence to say.

Example

> Student A: "What did you wash?"
> Student B: "My car."

1. a. What did you watch?   An old movie.
   b. What did you wash?   My car.

2. a. What does "chatter" mean?   To talk fast.
   b. What does "shatter" mean?   To break into small pieces.

3. a. What's a "chip"?   A small piece.
   b. What's a "ship"?   A big boat.

4. a. What does "cheap" mean?   Not expensive.
   b. What does "jeep" mean?   A car for rough roads.

5. a. What's a joke?   Something funny.
   b. What's a yolk?   The yellow part of an egg.

5. a. Her son went to Yale.   That's wonderful!
   b. Her son went to jail.   That's terrible!

6. a. What's Jell-O®?   A kind of dessert.
   b. What's yellow?   A banana.

7. a. What does "jell" mean?   To become solid.
   b. What does "yell" mean?   To shout.

K *Linking with /tʃ/ and /dʒ/*

1 Practice saying these words. Link the /tʃ/ and /dʒ/ sounds to
the vowel sound that comes next.

catch it	match everything	Judge Anderson
catchit	matcheverything	JudgeAnderson

watch us	fetch another	large office
charge us	reach over	

2 Practice linking in these sentences.

1. How can you watch every news program?
2. Try to catch it!
3. She wore a badge on her shirt.
4. The judge announced his choice.

L   *Music of English* 🎵🎶

1 Listen to these sentences and pay attention to the number of syllables in "oranges" and "wedges."

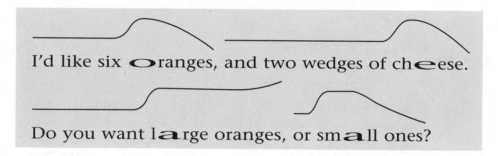

I'd like six **o**ranges, and two wedges of ch**e**ese.

Do you want l**a**rge oranges, or sm**a**ll ones?

2 Listen again. Practice the sentences until you can say them easily.

M   *The -es ending and the number of syllables* ☐☐☐

Many nouns and verbs end in the letters **-es**. In some words, the **-es** ending is pronounced as an extra syllable, but in other words it is not.

1 Listen to the following words that end in **-es**. In some of these words the **-es** ending adds an extra syllable, but in others it does not.

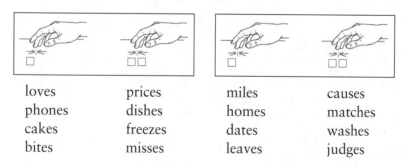

loves	prices	miles	causes
phones	dishes	homes	matches
cakes	freezes	dates	washes
bites	misses	leaves	judges

2 Do you know the rule for when the **-es** ending adds an extra syllable? If not, read the following clue.

Clue: Circle the words above that have a sibilant before the **-es** ending. How many syllables are in each word you circled?

3 Write down what you think the rule is for when to add an extra syllable with the **-es** ending. Check your answer on the last page of this unit.

Rule ....

N | Pair work: Sibilants and the number of syllables □ □ □

Student A: Say a word from each pair of words below.
Student B: Say the other word in the pair.

Take turns choosing a word to say.

Example

> Student A: "Washes."
> Student B: "Wash."

Note: In most English words, the letter **-x-** is pronounced as a combination of the sound **/k/** followed by the sound **/s/**. So words ending in **-x-**, like "mix" and "box," have a final sibilant sound.

Voiceless Sibilants

□	□□
wash	– washes
ice	– ices
dish	– dishes
watch	– watches
rich	– riches
mix	– mixes
tax	– taxes
box	– boxes

Voiced Sibilants

□	□□
rose	– roses
cause	– causes
buzz	– buzzes
badge	– badges
quiz	– quizzes
judge	– judges
page	– pages
prize	– prizes

O | Pair work: Singular or plural?

Student A: Say a sentence with either the singular or the plural form of the word in parentheses.
Student B: Say "singular" or "plural."

Example

> Student A: "The match fell on the floor."
> Student B: "Singular."

1. The (match / matches) fell on the floor.
2. Did you see the (prize / prizes)?

3. What (excuse / excuses) did he make?
4. Where did you put the (box / boxes)?
5. It depends on the (price / prices).
6. Did you wash the (dish / dishes)?
7. I put the (rose / roses) in water.
8. Which (sentence / sentences) did you write?

P *Pair work: Dialogue*

Listen. Then practice saying the dialogue with your partner.

Prizes

(A couple is talking at home. The wife has an idea, but her husband isn't very excited about it.)

Wife: Do you like surprises?
Husband: Sometimes. What is it?
Wife: We have a chance to win some great prizes.
Husband: How? Go on a TV quiz show?
Wife: You guessed it! I decided it would be fun.
Husband: I'm no good at quizzes.
Wife: But the second prize is a new watch!
Husband: I don't need any more watches.
Wife: And the first prize is a million dollars!
Husband: That's not so great. You have to pay a lot of taxes on prize money.

Q *Review: Linking with /ʃ/, /tʃ/, and /dʒ/*

Practice linking in these sentences. Say each sentence several times until the linked sounds seem like a new word.

1. The stain won't wash out.   shout

2. You can't catch air.   chair

3. How much does the judge owe?   Joe

🎧 R *Dictation*

Listen and write down the sentences you hear.

1. *Please don't put ice in my water.* ....
2. ....
3. ....
4. ....
5. ....

S *Check yourself: Sibilants and the number of syllables* ☐☐☐

1 If you have a tape recorder, record yourself reading these sentences.

> I'd like six oranges and two wedges of cheese. Oh . . . And may I have seven boxes of dates, please? One large and six small.

2 Listen to your recording, and check if you said the right number of syllables. Did you have three syllables for "oranges," two syllables for "wedges" and "boxes," and one syllable for "dates"?

VOWEL WORK

T *Difficult vowel contrasts*

The following vowel contrasts cause difficulty for some students. Choose the contrasts that you find most difficult, and practice saying those words.

tea /iʸ/	is /ɪ/		cake /eʸ/	ten /ɛ/		ten /ɛ/	pan /æ/		pan /æ/	top /a/
reach	rich		chase	chess		dead	dad		add	odd
steal	still		fade	fed		head	had		jab	job
feel	fill		shade	shed		then	than		stack	stock
heel	hill		age	edge		end	and		band	bond
we'll	will		tail	tell		lend	land		backs	box

Answer to Task M (page 126)

3 *Rule:* The **-es** ending adds an extra syllable only when it comes after a sibilant.

15 Thought groups

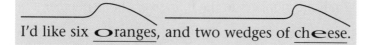

A Introducing thought groups

As you learned in Unit 6, English speakers use emphasis to help their listeners understand them. By using emphasis, you can help your listener to know which words are most important.

Another way that English speakers help their listeners to understand them is by separating words into *thought groups.*

A thought group is a group of words that belong together. A thought group can be a short sentence or part of a longer sentence. Each thought group has a focus word.

Listen. The following sentence has two thought groups. The underlined word in each thought group is the focus word.

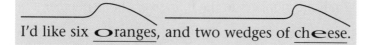

I'd like six **o**ranges, and two wedges of ch**ee**se.

Note: In written sentences, punctuation marks such as commas, periods, and question marks are often used to indicate the end of a thought group.

B Review of focus

- Focus words are emphasized to make them easier to hear.

- Focus words are emphasized by:
    1. Making the vowel in the stressed syllable extra long and clear
    2. Adding a pitch change to the stressed syllable

- Each thought group has a focus word.

C Signaling the end of a thought group with a pause

A *pause* gives listeners time to think about what was just said. If people have trouble understanding you, pausing at the end of each major thought group can help them to understand you better.

1 Listen to these sentences and notice how pauses are used between the thought groups.

1. I'd like six oranges, and two wedges of cheese.
2. When you get there, call me, and I'll come get you.
3. "Let's go for a walk," I said. But she replied, "I'm busy."

2 Practice saying the sentences. Pause after each thought group.

Thought Group Rule 1

There is often a pause at the end of a thought group to signal that the thought group is finished.

D   Using pauses with numbers

A pause is especially important when you are saying numbers (in addresses, telephone numbers, and so on). When numbers are written, each group is separated by a space or by punctuation marks, like parentheses or dashes. Notice how spaces and punctuation are used to group the numbers in the following phone number.

(415) 668-6963

In speech, pauses can be used to show how the numbers are grouped.

1 Listen to these numbers.

66-86963	six six	eight six nine six three
668-6963	six six eight	six nine six three

Did you hear the difference in grouping?

2 Practice saying the numbers above.

E   Pair work: Using pauses in phone numbers

Different countries group phone numbers differently. This is how phone numbers are grouped in North America:

Area code	Local code	Personal number
315	662	7131

1 Practice saying this phone number.

(315) 662-7131	three one five	six six two	seven one three one

2 Student A: Say phone number **a** or **b**. Be careful to pause at the
end of each group.

Student B: Write what you hear. Then check with your partner
to find out if you wrote the correct number.

1. a. (9164) 571-031
   b. (916) 457-1031   ....

2. a. (86) 636-94527
   b. (866) 369-4527   ....

3. a. (604) 60-84864
   b. (604) 608-4864   ....

3 Student A: Say your own telephone number to your partner.
Student B: Write what you hear.

Your partner's phone number: ....

Did you write the number with the correct grouping?

F   *Pair work: Using pauses in math problems*

Student A: Say math problem **a** or **b**. Be sure to pause at the end
of each group.

Student B: Circle the math problem that you hear. Then say the
correct answer.

Note: The correct answer depends on correct grouping.

Examples

Student A: (3 × 3) + 5 = what?

   three times three   plus five   equals what?

Student B: 14

Student A: 5 − (2 × 2) = what?

   five   minus two times two   equals what?

Student B: 1

Math problem	Answer
1. a. (3 × 3) + 5 = what?	14
b. 3 × (3 + 5) = what?	24
2. a. (5 − 2) × 2 = what?	6
b. 5 − (2 × 2) = what?	1
3. a. (4 − 1) × 3 = what?	9
b. 4 − (1 × 3) = what?	1
4. a. (10 − 1) × 2 = what?	18
b. 10 − (1 × 2) = what?	8
5. a. (4 + 2) × 3 = what?	18
b. 4 + (2 × 3) = what?	10
6. a. (2 × 2) + 3 = what?	7
b. 2 × (2 + 3) = what?	10

G Signaling the end of a thought group with a falling pitch

A *falling pitch* is another signal that a thought group is finished. Often a falling pitch and a pause are used together to signal the end of a thought group. When a speaker is talking quickly, however, there may not be time for a pause between thought groups. Then it is especially important to use a falling pitch.

1 Listen and repeat these sentences. Use a falling pitch as well as a pause to signal the end of each thought group.

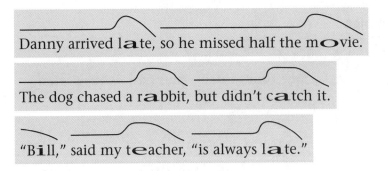

Danny arrived l**a**te, so he missed half the m**o**vie.

The dog chased a r**a**bbit, but didn't c**a**tch it.

"B**i**ll," said my t**e**acher, "is always l**a**te."

2 Practice these math problems again using a pause as well as falling pitch to signal the end of each group.

$(3 \times 3) + 5 = 14$ three times three   plus five   equals fourteen

$3 \times (3 + 5) = 24$ three   times three plus five   equals twenty four

---

Thought Group Rule 2

There is often a fall in pitch at the end of a thought group to signal that the thought group is finished.

Note: A big fall in pitch means the end of a sentence. A very big fall means the end of a person's turn to speak. At the end of a question, there may be a fall in pitch or a rise in pitch.

H   *Pair work: Signaling the end of a thought group*

Student A: Say sentence **a** or **b**. Then ask the question underneath the two sentences.

Student B: Respond with the appropriate answer on the right.

Example

> Student A: "'John,' said the boss, 'is absent.'"
>   "Who was speaking?"
> Student B: "The boss."

1. a. John said, "The boss is absent."   John.
   b. "John," said the boss, "is absent."   The boss.
      Question: Who was speaking?

2. a. Alfred said, "That clerk is incompetent!"   Alfred.
   b. "Alfred," said that clerk, "is incompetent!" That clerk.
      Question: Who was speaking?

3. a. The teacher said, "That student is lazy."   The teacher.
   b. "The teacher," said that student, "is lazy." That student.
      Question: Who was speaking?

4. a. Lisa said, "My dog is intelligent."   Lisa.
   b. "Lisa," said my dog, "is intelligent."   My dog.
      Question: Who is speaking?

I Either/or questions

Either/or questions offer a choice. Each choice belongs to a separate thought group. The pitch often rises on the first choice, but rises and falls on the second choice. This helps to make the two choices clear.

Listen to these either/or questions. Notice how the pitch rises on the first choice, and then rises and falls on the second choice. Also notice the pause between the two choices.

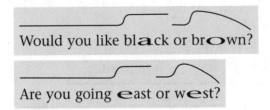

Would you like bl**a**ck or br**o**wn?

Are you going **e**ast or w**e**st?

J Asking either/or questions

Practice saying these questions. Let the pitch rise on the first choice, and then rise and fall on the second choice.

1. Would you like to work or rest?
2. Was the movie good or bad?
3. Is the chain silver or gold?
4. Will you go by bus or by train?
5. Do you want soup or salad?

K Series of items

When a sentence contains a series of items, each item is a separate thought. There is often a rise in pitch on each item in the series. But on the final item in the series, the pitch rises and then falls. That means "the end."

Listen to the following sentences. Notice how the pitch rises and falls on the last item in each series.

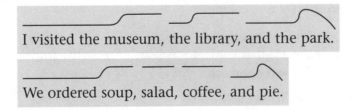

I visited the museum, the library, and the park.

We ordered soup, salad, coffee, and pie.

L Saying series of items

Practice saying these sentences. Be sure to let the pitch rise and fall on the last item in each series.

1. The shirt is red, blue, and green.
2. The pants are red, blue, green, and yellow.
3. They saw a Ford®, a Toyota®, and a Honda®.
4. We have a computer, a fax, and a scanner.
5. The zoo has elephants, tigers, bears, and lions.
6. His suitcase contains socks, ties, shirts, and some books.

M Pair work: Dialogue

1 Listen to the following dialogue, and make a slash (/) at the end of each thought group. Then underline the focus word in each thought group.

Difficult Children

Mother:	We want a turkey and cheese <u>sandwich,</u> /and two tuna sandwiches.
Server:	On white, whole wheat, or rye?
Mother:	The turkey and cheese on rye, and the other two on whole wheat.
First child:	No! No! I want white bread!
Mother:	Whole wheat's good for you.
Second child:	I want peanut butter and jelly, not tuna!
Mother:	OK. One turkey and cheese on rye, one tuna on white, and one peanut butter and jelly.
Server:	What would you like to drink?
Mother:	One iced tea, and two glasses of milk.
First child:	No milk! Lemonade!
Mother:	Three sandwiches, one iced tea, and two glasses of water.

2 Practice the dialogue with a partner. Use pauses and pitch to make the thought groups clear.

Pair work: Identifying thought groups

Student A: Say either sentence **a** or **b**. Then ask the question
           underneath the two sentences.
Student B: Respond with the appropriate answer on the right.

Example

Student A: "Do you want soup or salad?"
           "How many things were you offered?"
Student B: "Two."

1. a. Do you want a Super Salad?   One.
   b. Do you want a soup or salad?   Two.
      Question: How many things were you offered?

2. a. Jane said, "Is that Mister Fogg?"   A person.
   b. Jane said, "Is that mist or fog?"   The weather.
      Question: What was Jane asking about?

3. a. He sold his house, boat, and car.   Three.
   b. He sold his houseboat and car.   Two.
      Question: How many things did he sell?

4. a. She likes pie and apples.   Apples.
   b. She likes pineapples.   Pineapples.
      Question: What kind of fruit does she like?

5. a. We used wooden matches to start the fire.   One.
   b. We used wood and matches to start the fire.   Two.
      Question: How many things did they use?

6. a. She collects golden coins.   One.
   b. She collects gold and coins.   Two.
      Question: How many things did she collect?

7. a. When the water boils rapidly, put the   When the water
      spaghetti in the pot.   boils rapidly.
   b. When the water boils, rapidly put the   When the water
      spaghetti in the pot.   boils.
      Question: When should you put the spaghetti
                  in the pot?

O *Check yourself: Dialogue*

1 Read the following dialogue, and make a slash where you think each thought group ends. Then underline the focus word in each thought group.

2 Practice the dialogue with a partner. Remember to use pauses and pitch to make the thought groups clear.

Coffee Shop Confusion

(The customer doesn't hear very well, and the server is impatient.)

Customer: What can I have to start with?
Server: Soup or salad.
Customer: What's Super Salad?
Server: What do you mean, "Super Salad"?
Customer: Didn't you say you have a Super Salad?
Server: No, we don't have anything like that. Just plain green salad. Or you can start with tomato soup.
Customer: Oh, OK. Well, what do you have for dessert?
Server: We have ice cream, pie, and apples.
Customer: I don't like pineapples very much.
Server: Are you making jokes or what? We have ice cream, pie, and apples.
Customer: OK, OK. Just give me the soup and a piece of apple pie.
Server: Sorry, the only pie we have is berry.
Customer: Very what?
Server: Excuse me?
Customer: You said the pie was very something. Very good?
Server: I said the pie was berry – blackberry! And if you will wait just a minute, I'm going to get another server for you.

3 If you have a tape recorder, record the dialogue and then listen to it. Were the separate thought groups made clear? Were the focus words emphasized?

P   *Summary of focus and thought groups*

In the future, if someone has difficulty understanding what you have said, try following these steps.

1. Identify the focus words in what you just said.

2. Think about which syllable is stressed in each focus word.

3. Say the sentence(s) again, but make sure that you:

   • Lengthen the vowel in the stressed syllable of each focus word.

   • Make the sounds in the stressed syllable of each focus word very clear.

   • Change pitch on the stressed syllable of each focus word.

   • Group your words together in thought groups by using pitch changes (rises or falls) and by using pauses.

   • End complicated or especially important thought groups with an extra long pause, so the listener will have more time to think about what you just said.

Appendix A

Parts of the mouth

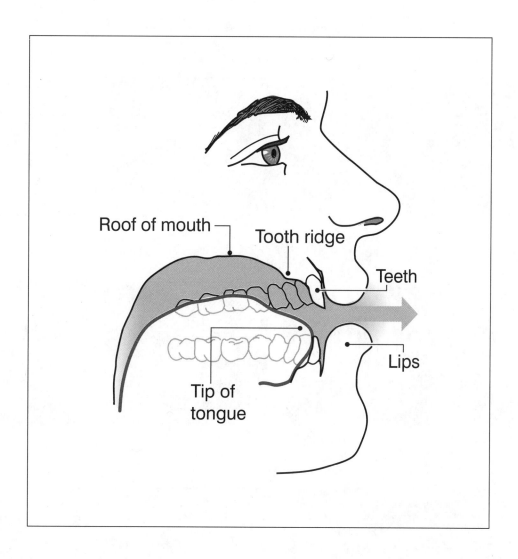

Roof of mouth

Tooth ridge

Teeth

Tip of tongue

Lips

Appendix B

Tongue shapes for /s/ and /z/, /t/ and /d/, /r/, /l/, /θ/ and /ð/

The photographs on the left show wax models. They are not real mouths.

Looking to the front

/s/ and /z/

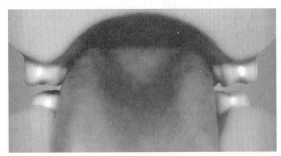 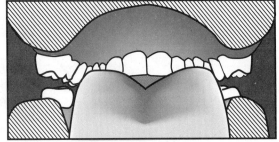

/t/ and /d/

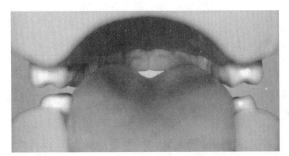 

/r/

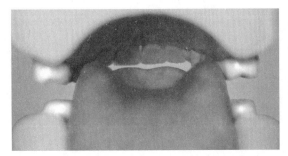 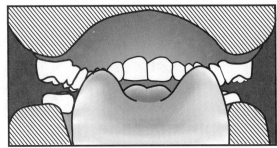

/l/

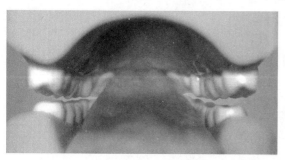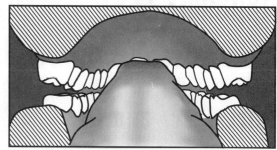

/θ/ and /ð/

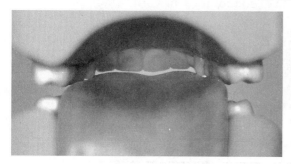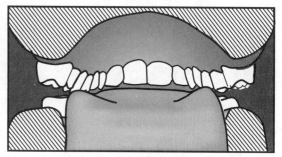

Appendix C

More consonant work

Part 1 /r/ and /l/

A *Listening to* /r/ *and* /l/

1 Listen and pay attention to the final sound in each word.

    car   call   mire   mile   fear   feel

2 Listen and pay attention to the beginning sound in each word.

    row   low   rhyme lime   rain   lane

B *Saying* /r/ *and* /l/

The sounds /r/ as in "fear" and /l/ as in "feel" are both continuants. When pronouncing /r/, air flows out along the middle of the tongue without stopping. For /l/, the tip of the tongue touches the tooth ridge at the front of the mouth, and air flows out each side.

1 Look at these pictures to see the differences between /r/ and /l/.

fear /r/

feel /l/

Looking from the side

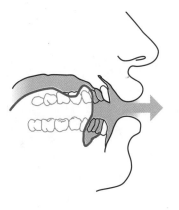

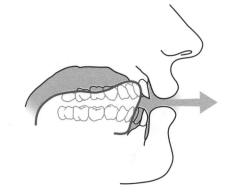

Looking to the front

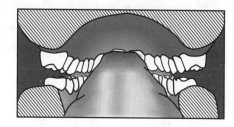

Looking down

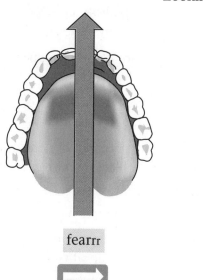 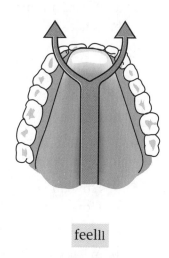

| fearrr | feelll |

2 Whisper the words "fear" and "feel" several times. Then practice saying them out loud.

C *Which word do you hear?*

1 Listen. Circle the word you hear.

Final sound		Beginning sound	
1. (roll)	roar	6. lock	rock
2. heal	hear	7. low	row
3. coal	core	8. late	rate
4. steel	steer	9. lamb	ram
5. fail	fair	10. lime	rhyme

2 Practice saying the words you circled.

D *Pair work: Saying /r/ and /l/ in sentences*

Student A: Ask question **a** or **b**.
Student B: Say the matching answer.

Example

> Student A: "What's a lamb?"
> Student B: "A baby sheep."

1. a. What's a ram?
   b. What's a lamb?

   A male sheep.
   A baby sheep.

2. a. Is it fall?
   b. Is it far?

   No, it's still summer.
   No, it's close.

3. a. Is it light?
   b. Is it right?

   No, it's heavy.
   No, it's wrong.

4. a. What does "core" mean?
   b. What does "coal" mean?

   The center, like the middle of an apple.
   A black rock that can burn.

5. a. How do you spell "loose"?
   b. How do you spell "ruse"?

   L - O - O - S - E.
   R - U - S - E.

6. a. What does "pale" mean?
   b. What does "pair" mean?

   Lacking color.
   A group of two.

7. a. How do you spell "lane"?
   b. How do you spell "rain"?

   L - A - N - E.
   R - A - I - N.

E *Linking with /r/ and /l/*

Practice linking with /**r**/ and /**l**/ in these sentences.

1. They moved far away.

   They moved farʳaway .

2. Park the car on the street.

   Park the carʳon the street.

3. Call everyone!

   Callˡeveryone !

4. How do you feel about this?

   How do you feelˡabout this?

F   _Poem with /r/ and /l/_

Practice saying this poem. Be careful to say the **/r/** and **/l/** sounds clearly.

The Crocodile

How doth the little crocodile
   Improve his shining tail,
And pour the waters of the Nile
   On every golden scale!

How cheerfully he seems to grin!
   How neatly spreads his claws,
And welcomes little fishes in
   With gently smiling jaws!

—Lewis Carroll

Note: "Doth" is an old word for "does." "Scales" are small bony flakes covering fish and reptiles.

Part 2 /n/ and /l/

A   _Listening to /n/ and /l/_

1 Listen to the final sound in each word.

   ten   tell   mine mile   win   will

2 Listen to the beginning sound in each word.

   no   low   night light   need   lead

B   _Saying /n/ and /l/_

The sounds **/n/** and **/l/** are both continuants. When saying the sound **/l/**, air flows out of the mouth around each side of the tongue. When saying the sound **/n/**, air does not flow out of the mouth. Instead, it flows out of the nose.

1 Look at these pictures and notice the differences in tongue position and airflow for the sounds /**n**/ and /**l**/.

ten /**n**/   tell /**l**/

Looking from the side

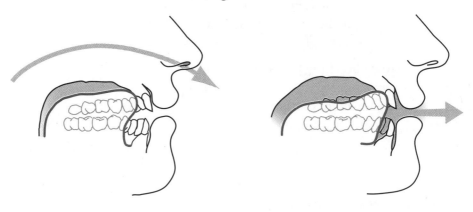

Looking to the front

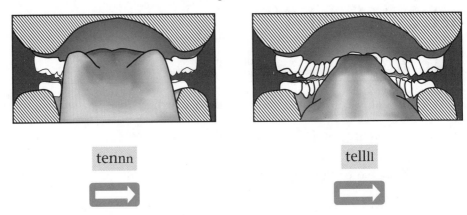

tennn   tellll

2 Practice the positions for /**n**/ and /**l**/. Then whisper the words "ten" and "tell" several times, paying attention to the difference in air flow for the final sounds.

3 Practice saying "ten" and "tell" out loud.

C The mirror test

You can use a mirror to check if you are saying the sounds /**n**/ and /**l**/ correctly.

1 If you have a small mirror, follow these steps.

1. Hold the mirror under your nose, and say the sound /**n**/ strongly.

2. Quickly look at the mirror, and you should see a cloud.

3. Say the sound /**l**/ and quickly look at the mirror. This time you should not see a cloud.

2 Try the mirror test with these words. Check your mirror after each word.

seen	seal
ten	tell
fine	file
rain	rail

D Which word do you hear?

1 Listen. Circle the word you hear.

Final sound		Beginning sound	
1. (pine)	pile	6. name	lame
2. cone	coal	7. nice	lice
3. main	mail	8. knife	life
4. when	well	9. niece	lease
5. tune	tool	10. not	lot

2 Practice saying the words you circled.

E Pair work: Saying /n/ and /l/ in sentences

Student A: Ask question **a** or **b**.
Student B: Say the matching answer.

Example

> Student A: "What does 'croon' mean?"
> Student B: "It's a kind of singing."

1. a. What does "croon" mean? It's a kind of singing.
   b. What does "cruel" mean? Unkind.

2. a. What's the opposite of "night"? Day.
   b. What's the opposite of "light"? Heavy.

3. a. How do you spell "snow"? S - N - O - W.
   b. How do you spell "slow"? S - L - O - W.

4. a. Can you define "snack"? Something to eat between meals.
   b. Can you define "slack"? It's the opposite of "tight."

5. a. What's a tool? A piece of equipment.
   b. What's a tune? A song.

F The sound combinations /n/ + /d/ and /l/ + /d/

Each of the following words ends in the sound combination
/**n**/ + /**d**/ or /**l**/ + /**d**/. Listen and repeat each pair of words. Be
careful to say the /**n**/ and /**l**/ sounds clearly.

/n/ + /d/	/l/ + /d/
find	filed
phoned	fold
trained	trailed
mind	mild
spend	spelled
found	fouled

G Linking with /n/, /l/, and /d/

Practice saying these sentences.

1. They can always go. They cannnalways go.
2. We call our dad every Sunday. We calllour dadevery Sunday.
3. We called our boss. We calledour boss.

4. When are you coming? Whennnare you coming?

5. Don't spend all our cash. Don't spendalllour cash.

Part 3 /v/ and /w/

A *Listening to* /v/ *and* /w/

Listen and pay attention to the beginning sound in each of these words.

vine wine veil whale vile while

B *Saying* /v/ *and* /w/

The sounds /v/ as in "vine" and /w/ as in "wine" are both continuants. When saying /v/, the upper teeth touch the back of the lower lip. For /w/ the lips are very rounded, and the teeth do not touch the lips at all.

1 Look at the pictures and notice the differences in teeth and lip position for the sounds /v/ and /w/.

vine /v/

wine /w/

Looking from the side

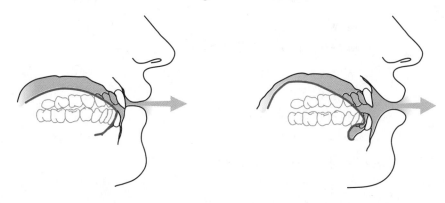

2 Practice alternating between the positions for /v/ and /w/. Then whisper the words "vine" and "wine" several times, paying close attention to the beginning sound in each word.

3 Practice saying "vine" and "wine" out loud.

Which word do you hear?

1 Listen. Circle the word you hear.

1. vile   (while)
2. vent   went
3. verse   worse
4. veal   wheel
5. vain   wane
6. vicious   wishes
7. -v-   we
8. vest   west

2 Practice saying the words you circled.

D *Pair work: Saying /v/ and /w/ in sentences*

Student A: Ask question **a** or **b**.
Student B: Say the matching answer.

Example

Student A: "What does 'vain' mean?" Student B: "Conceited."

1. a. What does "vain" mean?   Conceited.
   b. What does "wane" mean?   To get weaker.

2. a. Where's the wine?   In the bottle.
   b. Where's the vine?   On the fence.

3. a. How do you spell "whale"?   W - H - A - L - E.
   b. How do you spell "veil"?   V - E - I - L.

4. a. Where's the vest?   In the closet.
   b. Where's the West?   Opposite the East.

5. a. How do you spell "wishes"?   W - I - S - H - E - S.
   b. How do you spell "vicious"?   V - I - C - I - O - U - S.

6. a. Is he a very old man?   No, only 55.
   b. Is he a wary old man?   Yes, very suspicious.

7. a. What does "vile" mean?   Nasty.
   b. What does "while" mean?   A length of time.

Part 4 /v/ and /b/

A Listening to /v/ and /b/

1 Listen to the final sound in each of these words.

rove   robe   curve   curb

2 Listen to the beginning sound in each of these words.

vase   base   vote   boat

B Saying /v/ and /b/

The sound /v/ is a continuant and /b/ is a stop. When saying /v/, the upper teeth touch the back of the lower lip. The lips do not touch each other, and this allows air to flow out of the mouth. When saying /b/, the lips close, stopping the air inside the mouth.

1 Look at these pictures to see the differences between /v/ and /b/.

rove /v/   robe /b/

Looking from the side

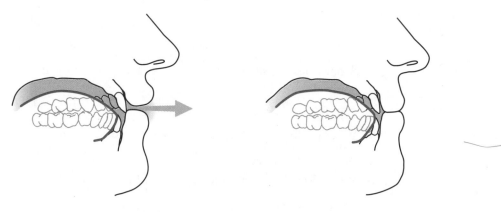

2 Silently try the positions for these two sounds.

Note: If you have trouble keeping your lips apart for the /v/ sound, place a pencil or your finger under your upper lip to remind you to keep the lips apart.

3 When you understand how the sounds are made, practice whispering the words "rove" and "robe." Then practice the words out loud.

C Which word do you hear?

1 Listen. Circle the word you hear.

Beginning sound		Final sound	
1. vase	(base)	7. rove	robe
2. vat	bat	8. curve	curb
3. very	berry	9. carve	carb
4. van	ban		
5. vest	best		
6. vote	boat		

2 Practice saying the words you circled.

D Pair work: Saying /v/ and /b/ in sentences

Student A: Say sentence **a** or **b**.
Student B: Say the matching response.

Example

> Student A: He wants to buy my vote.
> Student B: That's against the law!

1. a. He wants to buy my boat.   Will you sell it?
   b. He wants to buy my vote.   That's against the law!

2. a. What's a bat?   A stick used in baseball.
   b. What's a vat?   A big container for liquid.

3. a. What does "vest" mean?   It's a jacket with no sleeves.
   b. What does "best" mean?   The greatest.

4. a. Where's the vase?   On the table.
   b. Where's the base?   On the bottom.

5. a. What does "marvel" mean?   An amazing thing.
   b. What does "marble" mean?   A kind of stone.

6. a. What's a curve?   A bend.
   b. What's a curb?   The edge of a street.

E · Linking with /v/ and /b/ ⊂⊃⊂⊃⊂⊃⊂⊃⊂⊃

Practice linking with /v/ and /b/ in these sentences.

1. Will you leave early?   Will you leavvvearly ?
2. Have a bite.   Havvva bite.
3. Can you believe it?   Can you believvvit ?
4. Don't rob us!   Don't robus !
5. Join the club again.   Join the clubagain .
6. It won't rub off.   It won't ruboff .

F · Pair work: Dialogue

Practice this dialogue with a partner.

The Great Athlete

A: Do you like to play volleyball?
B: Not very much.
A: But it's fun!
B: I can't serve the ball.
A: You just have to keep working at it.
B: But I never get the ball over the net.
A: Never?
B: Well, hardly ever. Besides that, I always bump into the other players.
A: Hmm. Then maybe you'd better try bowling.

Part 5 /f/ and /p/

A · Listening to /f/ and /p/

Listen and hear the difference between these words.

leaf   leap   coffee   copy   fool   pool

B *Saying /f/ and /p/*

1 Look at these pictures for the continuant sound /**f**/ and the stop sound /**p**/. The teeth, tongue, and lip positions for these sounds are the same as for /**v**/ and /**b**/, but /**f**/ and /**p**/ are voiceless.

lea**f** /**f**/   leap /**p**/

Looking from the side

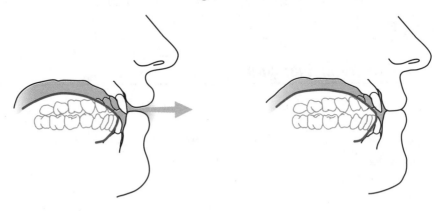

2 Silently practice the positions for /**f**/ and /**p**/. Then whisper the words "leaf" and "leap" several times.

3 Practice saying "leaf" and "leap" out loud.

C *Which word do you hear?*

1 Listen. Circle the word you hear.

Beginning sound		Final sound	
1. fool	(pool)	7. laugh	lap
2. fast	past	8. wife	wipe
3. foot	put	9. cliff	clip
4. foal	pole	10. leaf	leap
5. fat	pat		
6. face	pace		

2 Practice saying the words you circled.

D   *Pair work: Saying /f/ and /p/ in sentences*

Student A: Say sentence **a** or **b**.
Student B: Say the matching response.

Example

> Student A: "Where's the pan?"
> Student B: "In the kitchen cabinet."

1. a. Where's the fan?   On the ceiling.
   b. Where's the pan?   In the kitchen cabinet.

2. a. What's the opposite of "fail"?   "Succeed."
   b. What's the opposite of "pale"?   "Bright and colorful."

3. a. What's a fool?   A silly person.
   b. What's a pool?   A place to swim.

4. a. What's a foal?   A baby horse.
   b. What's a pole?   A long stick.

5. a. How do you spell "wife"?   W - I - F - E.
   b. How do you spell "wipe"?   W - I - P - E.

6. a. How do you spell "lab"?   L - A - B.
   b. How do you spell "laugh"?   L - A - U - G - H.

7. a. The copy machine doesn't work.   Call the technician.
   b. The coffee machine doesn't work.   I guess I'll have tea.

E   *Linking with /f/ and /p/*

Practice linking with /**f**/ and /**p**/ in these sentences.

1. There's a leaf in your hair.   There's a leafffin your hair.

2. If it fits, I'll wear it.   Ifffit fits, I'll wear it.

3. Stuff all the clothes in this bag.   Stufffall the clothes in this bag.

4. Leap over the fence.   Leapover the fence.

5. Clip important articles.   Clipimportant articles.

6. I like to sleep until seven.   I like to sleepuntil seven.

Part 6 /θ/ (bath) and /t/ (bat)

A Listening to /θ/ (bath) and /t/ (bat)

1 Listen to the final sound in each of these words.

bath   bat   both   boat

2 Listen to the beginning sound in each of these words.

thank   tank   thought   taught

B Saying /θ/ and /t/

The sound /θ/ as in "bath" is a continuant, and the sound /t/ as in "bat" is a stop.

1 Look at these pictures of /θ/ and /t/ and notice how the air flows out of the mouth for /θ/, but stops inside the mouth for /t/.

bath /θ/   bat /t/

Looking from the side

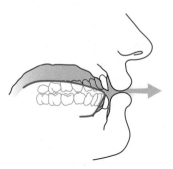   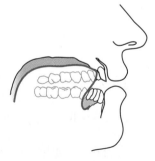

Looking to the front

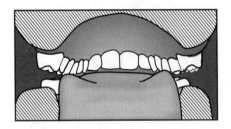   

When saying /θ/, the tongue is flat and relaxed. The flat tip of the tongue briefly touches the upper front teeth. You can also make this sound by touching the tip of the tongue to the lower front teeth. Either way, the air must continue to flow out of the mouth.

2 Silently practice the position for /θ/. Breathe out and feel the air moving quietly over the tongue and teeth. If you draw the air back into your mouth, you can feel the cold air over your flat tongue.

3 Raise your tongue and press it against the tooth ridge all around so that the air cannot flow out. This makes the stop sound /t/.

4 Silently change back and forth between the positions for the two sounds. Then practice saying the words "bath" and "bat" out loud.

C *Which word is different?*

Listen. You will hear three words. Mark the column for the word that is different.

	X	Y	Z	
1.	....	....	✔.............	(bath, bath, bat)
2.	....	....	....	
3.	....	....	....	
4.	....	....	....	
5.	....	....	....	
6.	....	....	....	
7.	....	....	....	
8.	....	....	....	

D *Pair work: Saying words with final /θ/ and /t/*

Student A: Say one word from each pair of words.
Student B: Pay close attention to the final sound in the word, and say "stop" or "continuant."

Example

> Student A: "Bath."
> Student B: "Continuant."

1.	bath	bat
2.	both	boat
3.	booth	boot
4.	faith	fate
5.	Ruth	root
6.	math	mat
7.	wrath	rat

E Saying sentences with /θ/ and /t/

Student A: Say sentence **a** or **b**.
Student B: Say the matching response.

Example

> Student A: "What does 'path' mean?"
> Student B: "A little road."

1. a. What does "path" mean?   A little road.
   b. What does "pat" mean?   To tap.

2. a. What's a bath for?   To get clean.
   b. What's a bat for?   To play ball.

3. a. How do you spell "both"?   B - O - T - H.
   b. How do you spell "boat"?   B - O - A - T.

4. a. What does "faith" mean?   Belief.
   b. What does "fate" mean?   Destiny.

5. a. How do you spell "mat"?   M - A - T.
   b. How do you spell "math"?   M - A - T - H.

6. a. Define "wrath."   It means anger.
   b. Define "rat."   It's like a big mouse.

7. a. Where is the booth?   At the fair.
   b. Where is the boot?   On my foot.

8. a. How do you spell "Ruth"?   R - U - T - H.
   b. How do you spell "root"?   R - O - O - T.

Part 7 Silent -t- and reduced -t-

A Silent -t-

When the phrases "want to" and "going to" are said quickly, the "to" is often reduced so much that the letter -t- is silent. When "want to" is said quickly, it often sounds like "wanna." When "going to" is said quickly, it often sounds like "gonna."

Note: You do not need to use this reduction when you speak English, but you should learn to recognize it in other people's speech.

Listen to these sentences and mark the column labeled "Slow and extra careful" or "Fast and reduced."

	Slow and extra careful	Fast and reduced
1. We want to go on a trip.	....	✔
2. I want to buy a car.	....	....
3. They want to buy a present.	....	....
4. I think they're going to leave.	....	....
5. Are you going to show us your work?	....	....
6. What are you going to do now?	....	....
7. I want to study now.	....	....
8. Why do you want to work so hard?	....	....
9. Because I want to succeed.	....	....
10. Do you want to be rich?	....	....

B Reduced -t- between vowels

At the end of a stressed syllable, the letter -t- is often reduced to a quick /d/ sound when it is followed by a vowel. For example, the word "liter" sounds like "leader," and the word "atom" sounds like "Adam."

Note: It is not important for you to use the reduced -t- in your own speech, but practicing to say the reduced -t- will help you to hear it accurately when you listen to other speakers.

Practice using a quick /d/ sound for the letter -t- in the following words and phrases.

later	atom
water	great ending
better	short answer
liter	hit another
hotter	write in
city	get us

Part 8 Aspiration

A *Introducing aspiration*

At the beginning of a word, voiceless stop sounds (/**p**/, /**t**/, and /**k**/) are always followed by a puff of air. This puff of air is called *aspiration*. Voiced stops (/**b**/, /**d**/, and /**g**/) are never aspirated.

By adding aspiration to the voiceless stops at the beginning of words, you will help others to understand you more easily. Aspiration may even be more important than voicing in helping others to recognize a stop at the beginning of a word.

Practice saying the following pairs of words. Make a puff of air after the voiceless stops, but not after the voiced stops.

Note: You can check yourself by saying each word with a thin piece of paper in front of your lips. The paper will move if there is an extra puff of air. You can also feel the air if you hold your hand in front of your mouth.

Voiceless stop /p/	Voiced stop /b/
1. pay	bay
2. pan	ban
3. pea	bee
4. pole	bowl
5. peach	beach

Voiceless stop /t/	Voiced stop /d/
6. tab	dab
7. tank	dank
8. teen	dean
9. ten	den
10. tied	died

Voiceless stop /k/	Voiced stop /g/
11. cap	gap
12. cave	gave
13. coast	ghost
14. curl	girl
15. card	guard

B Aspiration in sentences

Student A: Say sentence **a** or **b**.
Student B: Say the matching response.

Be sure to make a puff of air for each voiceless stop at the beginning of a stressed syllable.

Example

> Student A: "Where's the peach?"
> Student B: "In the fruit bowl."

1. a. Where's the peach?   In the fruit bowl.
   b. Where's the beach?   By the ocean.

2. a. Define "tank."   A container for liquid.
   b. Define "dank."   It means cold, wet, and unpleasant.

3. a. What does "tense" mean?   Under stress.
   b. What does "dense" mean?   Very thick.

4. a. Where's the card?   In my desk.
   b. Where's the guard?   Standing at the door.

5. a. How do you spell "could"?   C - O - U - L - D.
   b. How do you spell "good"?   G - O - O - D.

6. a. Define "cause."   A reason for something.
   b. Define "gauze."   Thin cotton cloth.

7. a. How do you spell "ghost"?   G - H - O - S - T.
   b. How do you spell "coast"?   C - O - A - S - T.

C Aspiration in multi-syllable words

At the beginning of a stressed syllable, voiceless stops are always aspirated.

The stressed syllable in each word below begins with a voiceless stop. Practice saying the words. Be sure to make a puff of air after each stop at the beginning of a stressed syllable.

/p/	/t/	/k/
popular	tension	casual
pencil	toasted	coffee
appear	attend	accuse
apartment	attempt	account
report	return	recall
unpopular	eternal	uncover

Part 9 Practice with linking

A Review: Linking with stops

Practice linking stops to vowels in the following sentences.

1. We made other plans.
2. Lock all the doors.
3. Stop it now!
4. They got away.
5. Rob always goes.
6. I'll bet it doesn't fit anymore.
7. Dave bought a bag of chips.
8. Would anyone like a cup of tea?

B Review: Linking with continuants

Practice linking with continuants in the following sentences.

1. This is a space age project.
2. That's a fair answer.
3. You can't have both of them.
4. We can always share a taxi.
5. He'll always be there for you.
6. There's a fly in this ice!
7. Please answer the question honestly.
8. I'm never there on Saturdays.

C Linking with the same continuant sound

When you link two continuant sounds that are the same, do not say the sound twice. Instead, say the sound once, but make it longer.

1 Practice saying these linked words.

bus system	half full	team member
busssystem	halffffull	teammmmember
wash shells	call Lisa	have vitamins
we're ready	all leather	plan nothing

2 Practice linking in these sentences. Do not pause between the linked words.

1. Pam might go.   Pammmmight go.
2. The sun never rises.   The sunnnneverrrrises.
3. Bill loves to dance.   Billlloves to dance.
4. We both think it's beautiful.
5. I wish she'd come.

Appendix D

Advanced tasks

Part 1 Word stress

A *Pair work: Practice with syllable number*

Student A: Ask question **a** or **b**.
Student B: Say the matching answer.

Example

> Student A: "What's the train like?"
> Student B: "It's fast and loud."

1. a. What's the te**rrain** like? Very bumpy.
   b. What's the **train** like? It's fast and loud.

2. a. What does "**sport**" mean? A game, like football.
   b. What does "su**pport**" mean? Something like "help."

3. a. What color is "**rust**"? Reddish brown.
   b. What color is "**russ**et"? More brown than red.

4. a. How do you spell "**sett**ing"? S - E - T - T - I - N - G.
   b. How do you spell "**sting**"? S - T - I - N - G.

5. a. How do you spell "**fast**"? F - A - S - T.
   b. How do you spell "**fac**et"? F - A - C - E - T.

6. a. What does "**tenn**is" mean? A sport with rackets.
   b. What does "**tense**" mean? In this class, it's a grammar word.

7. a. What does "**planned**" mean? The past tense of "plan."
   b. What does "**plan**et" mean? A thing that goes around the sun.

8. a. Was it **wrapped**? Yes, in wrapping paper.
   b. Was it **rap**id? No, very slow.

9. a. What does "**stamped**" mean? The past tense of "stamp."
   b. What does "stam**pede**" mean? A lot of animals running.

B Descriptive phrases and compound words

When an adjective comes just before a noun in a two-word descriptive phrase, the second word of the phrase (the noun) is stressed.

Adjective		Noun		Descriptive phrase
green	+	house	=	green **house** (a house that is green)

However, when an adjective and a noun are combined to form a compound word, the stress is always on the first part of the compound word (the adjective).

Adjective		Noun		Compound word
green	+	house	=	**green**house (a glass building used for growing plants)

Practice saying the following compound words and descriptive phrases with the correct stress patterns. The stressed syllables are in bold.

	Descriptive phrase		Compound word	
1.	the white **house**	(a house that is white)	the **White** House	(the U.S. President's house)
2.	a white **board**	(a board that is white)	a **white**board	(used for writing in class)
3.	a black **bird**	(a bird that is black)	a **black**bird	(a specific type of bird)
4.	a hot **dog**	(a warm animal)	a **hot**dog	(something to eat)
5.	a dark **room**	(a room without light)	a **dark**room	(a place to develop film)

C Pair work: Saying stressed syllables in sentences

If you say words using their correct stress pattern, it is easier for other people to understand you, even if you do not get all the sounds exactly right.

Student A: Ask question **a** or **b**.
Student B: Say the matching answer.

Example

> Student A: "What did you think of the committee?"
> Student B: "They're writing a good report."

1. a. What did you think of the com**mitt**ee? They're writing a good report.
   b. What did you think of the **com**edy? It wasn't very funny.

2. a. What does "**el**igible" mean? Qualified.
   b. What does "il**leg**ible" mean? Unreadable.

3. a. Does she want a **need**le? Yes, to sew on a new button.
   b. Does she want **an**y doll? No, she wants a special one.

4. a. What does "**es**timator" mean? A person who figures costs.
   b. What does "a **steam** motor" mean? A motor that uses steam.

5. a. Do the students like **his**tory? No, there are too many dates.
   b. Do the students like his **stor**y? Yes, it's funny.

6. a. How do you spell "**dep**uty"? D - E - P - U - T - Y.
   b. How do you spell "the **beau**ty"? As two words.

7. a. Is it ele**men**tary? No, it's advanced.
   b. Is it a **lem**on tree? No, it's an orange tree.

8. a. What's for **rain**? An umbrella.
   b. What's **for**eign? Another language.

9. a. Is that **Eu**rope? No, it's Asia.
   b. Is that your **rope**? No, it's hers.

10. a. What's in the **des**ert? Lots of sand.
    b. What's in the de**ssert**? Lots of sugar.

Part 2 Sentence focus

A Pair work: Focus words and the meaning of emphasis

Student A: Say sentence **a** or **b**. Be sure to emphasize the focus word.
Student B: Listen closely for the focus word and say the most likely meaning of the sentence.

Example

> Student A: "We want three tickets for to**day's** show."
> Student B: "Not tomorrow's show."

1. a. We want **three** tickets for today's show. Not two.
   b. We want three tickets for to**day's** show. Not tomorrow's show.

2. a. Please give me **both** books. Not just one.
   b. **Please** give me both books. I want them very much.

3. a. I didn't know she was out **there**.   I thought she was somewhere else.

   b. I didn't know **she** was out there.   I thought it was someone else.

4. a. I **think** I paid five dollars.   I'm not sure.
   b. I think I paid **five** dollars.   Not ten.

5. a. I told **you** about that.   I didn't tell anyone else.
   b. I **told** you about that.   Don't you remember?

6. a. Gary **lives** here.   He's not just visiting.
   b. Gary lives **here**.   Not somewhere else.

7. a. We ordered **coff**ee!   Not tea.
   b. **We** ordered coffee!   It wasn't them.

B   *Pair work: Focus words in a dialogue*

1 Working alone, underline the focus words in this dialogue.

2 Take turns reading the dialogue out loud to your partner. As you listen to your partner, circle the words your partner emphasizes.

Note: You and your partner do not have to agree on your choice of focus words, but you do have to make your choice of focus words clear by emphasizing them with a pitch change and a long, clear vowel in the stressed syllable.

New York Cab Ride

Driver: Where to?
Passenger: Times Square, please.
Driver: Where are you visiting from?
Passenger: Chicago.
Driver: Yeah, that's what I thought, from the accent.
Passenger: Really? I have an accent? Funny, I never thought about it. Where are you from?
Driver: Atlanta.
Passenger: Really? You're from the South? You don't sound southern.
Driver: No, of course not. I'm studying to be an actor, and you can't have any accent if you want to be an actor.
Passenger: So you just got rid of your southern accent?
Driver: That's right. I wiped it out completely.
Passenger: That's really interesting. I guess that's why you sound like you're from New York.
Driver: I do?

C *Pair work: Checking information*

In the following dialogues, Speaker B emphasizes a question word
("how," "what," "why," etc.) to find out what Speaker A said.
This is a useful way to ask about something you did not
understand or did not hear clearly.

A: Millie let the cat out!
B: **Who** did?
A: Millie.

A: The sandwich was made with goat cheese.
B: **What** kind of cheese?
A: Goat cheese.

1 Read each dialogue. Write a question for Speaker B that makes
sense with Speaker A's final answer.

  1. A: We need tomatoes for the sauce.
      B: *What do we need* ?
      A: Tomatoes.

  2. A: Tom needs a new battery for his car.
      B: ?
      A: Tom.

  3. A: The travel agent made a mistake in our arrangements.
      B: ?
      A: The travel agent.

  4. A: Melissa is coming at five o'clock.
      B: ?
      A: Five.

  5. A: We went to the airport by bus.
      B: ?
      A: To the airport.

  6. A: Richard has a mountain of books on his desk.
      B: ?
      A: On his desk.

  7. A: You need a badge to get into the building.
      B: ?
      A: A badge.

  8. A: Mr. Johnson forgot to sign his name.
      B: ?
      A: Mr. Johnson.

2 Practice reading the dialogues out loud with your partner.

D   *Pair work: What was the question?*

When listening to a conversation, you may not hear everything that is said. For example, you may hear a speaker's response without hearing the question that came before it. When this happens, if you listen closely to the emphasis in the response, you may be able to guess what the question was.

1 Read the dialogues below and fill in Speaker A's missing question. Then compare your questions with your partner. Your questions may not be exactly the same, but they should make sense with Speaker B's final answer.

1. A: When does the train leave?
   B: At seven.
   A: *Seven in the morning* ?
   B: No, in the **eve**ning.

2. A: When will you begin your vacation?
   B: In June.
   A: ?
   B: No, at the **end** of June.

3. A: How much will a ticket cost?
   B: Twenty dollars.
   A: ?
   B: No, **twen**ty.

4. A: What are those people doing?
   B: They're planting a garden.
   A: ?
   B: A **veg**etable garden.

5. A: What's the play about?
   B: The Revolution.
   A: ?
   B: No, the **French** Revolution.

2 Practice reading the dialogues out loud with your partner.

E *What will come next?*

Using correct emphasis when you speak can help your listener to predict what you will say next. This will make it easier for your listener to follow what you are saying.

1 Read the unfinished sentences below and predict what the speaker will say next. Write an ending to each sentence, and underline the word or words that should be emphasized (the focus word) in the part that you wrote.

1. We had a lot of rain **last** year, but *not much this year*
2. I don't like to **write**, but
3. **This** pen doesn't write very well, but
4. To**ma**toes are expensive, but
5. My **sis**ter got a raise in pay, but
6. Brian is really **tall**, but

2 Practice saying the sentences, being careful to emphasize only the focus words.

Part 3 Thought groups

A *Road signs*

Road signs are words or phrases that tell your listener that you will either continue talking about the same idea or that you are going to change direction. In other words, road signs let your listener know where you are headed, so that the listener can follow what you are saying.

Road signs are important signals. They should be said with a pitch change and a pause, so that the listener will notice them.

1 The following words and phrases tell the listener that the speaker will continue in the same direction.

first of all	secondly	moreover	and then
besides	as a result	consequently	so
furthermore	in the same way		

2 Read these sentences and notice how road signs are used to guide the listener.

First of all, you should be well prepared.

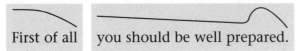

Secondly, it's essential that you arrive on time.

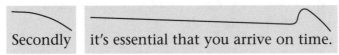

3 The following words and phrases tell the listener that the speaker will not continue in the same direction, but will change direction.

however	instead	on the contrary	in contrast
but	nevertheless	on the other hand	

4 Notice how a road sign is used in this sentence.

However, if you really can't be on time, have a good excuse.

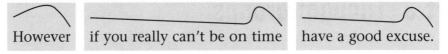

5 The following words and phrases let the listener know that the speaker is about to finish.

lastly	finally	to sum up
all in all	in conclusion	

6 Read this sentence and notice how a road sign is used.

Lastly, don't miss more than three classes.

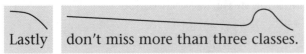

7 Practice reading the following paragraph out loud. Be sure to separate the thought groups clearly. Be extra careful to use pitch changes and pauses with the road signs.

> First of all, you should be well prepared. Secondly, It's essential that you arrive on time. However, if you really can't be on time, have a good excuse. Lastly, don't miss more than three classes.

B Pair work: Monologue

1 Read the following story and separate the thought groups with a slash (/). Remember to draw a slash after each road sign.

2 Underline the words that should be emphasized (the focus words) in each thought group.

A Bad Day

This has been the most terrible day! Everything went wrong! First of all, I couldn't find my keys. Then, I knew I was going to be late to work, so I drove too fast, and a cop gave me a speeding ticket. When the officer asked for my driver's license, I realized that I had left it at home! As a result, the fine will be even higher. After that, I got a flat tire and had to change it, which took even more time. Finally, when I arrived at work, I remembered that it was a holiday, and the office was closed!

3 Take turns listening to each other tell the story. Did you emphasize the focus words? Did you use pitch changes and pauses to help the listener follow the story? Could you recognize the pitch changes and pauses when your partner was telling the story?

C Parenthetical remarks

Parenthetical remarks carry information that is less important. In writing, they are marked by parentheses, dashes, or commas. In speech, they are usually said at a lower pitch and marked by pauses on either side.

Read the following sentences with the pitch pattern shown.

1. Students, of course, should be well prepared.

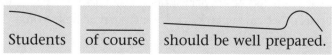

2. Unprepared students (naturally) get less out of their classes.

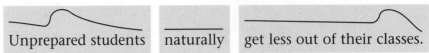

| Unprepared students | naturally | get less out of their classes. |

3. They find – to their surprise – that effort does pay off.

| They find | to their surprise | that effort does pay off. |

D Pair work: Road signs and parenthetical remarks

1 Underline the road signs and the parenthetical remarks in the following passage.

Preparing for a Job Interview

A job interview, as you probably know, can be a pretty stressful experience. However, there are several things you can do to help insure that an interview will run smoothly.

First of all, prepare yourself by learning as much as you can about the job you are applying for. Look for information about the company or organization online, for example, or speak to others who work in the same field.

Secondly, make a list of your relevant skills and experiences. Write down those things you have learned in school, for instance, or in other jobs that will help you to be successful in the position you hope to fill. Then, try to memorize the skills and experiences you listed, so that you can refer to them easily during the interview.

On the day of the interview, leave yourself more than enough time to get there. You should try to arrive early or, at the very least, get there on time. After all, you do not want to rush into the meeting or, even worse, arrive late.

Finally, try not to be nervous. This, of course, is the hardest step of all. However, if you have made an effort to prepare yourself adequately, then you have every reason to approach the interview with complete confidence.

2 Take turns reading the passage out loud to your partner. Be sure to use pauses and the appropriate pitch changes with each road sign and parenthetical remark. Did your partner hear your pauses and pitch changes?

Appendix E

How often do the vowel rules work?

How often does the Two Vowel Rule work?

Letters	Sounds	Percent of time[1]	Examples
-ai -a- + final -e- -ay	/e^y/	95% 90% 93%	rain, train, afraid cake, came, arrange day, say, play, array
-e- + final -e- -ee- -ea- -y	/i^y/	32% 92% 69% 95%	Pete, athlete, recede tree, meet, agreement tea, please, beat, season city, funny, lucky
-i- + final -e- -igh-*	/a^y/	77% 100%	ice, time, white, arrive night, light, high, sigh
-o- + final -e- -oa- -ow-	/o^w/	76% 94% 53%	cone, home, alone coat, soap, approach slow, below, lower, follow
-u- + final -e- -oo-*	/u^w/	94% 88%	blue, juice, accuse room, choose, foolish

How often does the One Vowel Rule work?

Letters	Sounds	Percent of time[1]	Examples
-a-	/æ/	91%	pan, has, aspirin, answer
-e-	/ɛ/	82%	ten, message, medicine, intention
-i-	/ɪ/	93%	is, simple, children, interesting
-o-	/ɑ/	74%	top, hot, problem, confident
-u-	/ʌ/	66%	cup, sun, butter, hundred, assumption

[1] These numbers refer to the percentage of times that this spelling produces this vowel sound, based on multi-syllabic words in a database formed by merging five very large independent American and British frequency counts, including approximately 25 million words of text. (Carney, 1994, p. 104)

* This common spelling does not follow the Two Vowel Rule, but it is included here because it is so often pronounced with the sound shown.

Track listing for Student Audio CD

Track	Unit	Task
1	1	A
2	1	C
3	1	D
4	1	K
5	1	M
6	1	O
7	2	B
8	2	E
9	2	I
10	2	J
11	2	O
12	2	P
13	2	S
14	3	C
15	3	D
16	3	E
17	3	I
18	4	C
19	4	D
20	4	F
21	4	H
22	4	L
23	5	B
24	5	F
25	5	G
26	5	H
27	5	J
28	5	N

Track	Unit	Task
29	6	B
30	6	D
31	6	G
32	7	F
33	7	G
34	7	H
35	7	I
36	7	K
37	8	A
38	8	C
39	8	E
40	8	K
41	8	M
42	9	B
43	9	H
44	9	K
45	9	L
46	9	M
47	10	C
48	10	D
49	10	E
50	10	I
51	10	J
52	11	C
53	11	D
54	11	F
55	11	G
56	11	H

Track	Unit	Task
57	11	K
58	11	N
59	11	O
60	11	Q
61	12	A
62	12	B
63	12	C
64	12	F
65	12	I
66	12	L
67	12	P
68	12	U
69	13	A
70	13	B
71	13	F
72	13	N
73	14	A
74	14	C
75	14	D
76	14	I
77	14	L
78	15	C
79	15	D
80	15	G
81	15	I
82	15	K